THE
SHEPHERD'S CALENDAR

JOHN CLARE

THE SHEPHERD'S CALENDAR

EDITED BY ERIC ROBINSON
GEOFFREY SUMMERFIELD AND DAVID POWELL

With wood engravings by David Gentleman

Second Edition

Oxford   New York

OXFORD UNIVERSITY PRESS

Oxford University Press, Walton Street, Oxford OX2 6DP
Oxford New York Toronto
Delhi Bombay Calcutta Madras Karachi
Kuala Lumpur Singapore Hong Kong Tokyo
Nairobi Dar es Salaam Cape Town
Melbourne Auckland Madrid

and associated companies in
Berlin Ibadan

Oxford is a trade mark of Oxford University Press

This edition © Oxford University Press 1964, 1973, 1993

First published 1964 by Oxford University Press
First issued as an Oxford University Press paperback 1973
Reprinted eight times
Second edition first published 1993

British Library Cataloguing in Publication Data
Data available

Library of Congress Cataloging in Publication Data
Clare, John, 1793–1864.
The shepherd's calendar / John Clare; edited by Eric Robinson,
Geoffrey Summerfield, and David Powell; with wood engravings by
David Gentleman.—2nd ed.
p.   cm.   Includes bibliographical references.
1. Pastoral poetry, English.   I. Robinson, Eric, 1924–
II. Summerfield, Geoffrey.   III. Powell, David, 1925–
IV. Title.
821'.7—dc20   PR4453.C6S45   1993   92-44091
ISBN 0-19-283154-2

3 5 7 9 10 8 6 4

Printed in Great Britain by
Biddles Ltd
Guildford and King's Lynn

ACKNOWLEDGMENTS

THIS book was prepared with the assistance of a National Endowment for the Humanities Grant (Editions), and with the help of the British Academy and the Leverhulme Foundation.

Mr John Bell of Wootton, near Woodstock, now retired from Oxford University Press, was the editor who commissioned the earlier edition of this book in 1964. He listened to the views of two young editors, helped them to choose the illustrator, David Gentleman, and paid attention to their preferences in typography and layout. He recommended the book to the Oxford Printer and this resulted in the award of the bronze medallion for the most beautifully produced book of the year at the Leipzig World Book Fair in 1964. No one could have been more professional, more enthusiastic or more civil. He has had an important part in establishing John Clare's reputation.

The general reader may wish to know about the John Clare Society (Secretary: Mrs Mary Moyse, The Stables, 1A West Street, Helpston, Peterborough, PE6 7DU. Telephone 0733 252678) which has provided us with a forum and which works hard to make Clare better known.

The editors want to thank all the librarians and curators who have made their work possible—especially the staffs of the Peterborough Museum and Peterborough Museum Society, the Northampton

ACKNOWLEDGMENTS

Central Public Library, the British Library, the Berg Collection and the Pforzheimer Collection in the New York Public Library, the Pierpont Morgan Library, and many other institutions.

Most of all we want to thank other scholars—Professors R. K. R. Thornton and Mark Storey of Birmingham University, the late Dr Margaret Grainger, the late Professor J. W. and Mrs Anne Tibble, and last and certainly not least, the late Geoffrey Summerfield himself, who, with Eric Robinson, began the venture of editing Clare some thirty years ago. We shall miss his enthusiasm for Clare and his great qualities as a teacher. He shared with Clare a great love of children and of childhood.

E.R.
D.P.

CONTENTS

INTRODUCTION

ACCORDING to Mark Storey, 'Clare's idea of the true pastoral was to consist of his own *Shepherd's Calendar*',[1] and it is certainly his most widely-read work, despite the fact that it sold only a few copies when it was first published in 1827. Since Geoffrey Summerfield and I brought out our edition of the poem in 1964, over five thousand copies have been sold: the poem has had several readings, complete as well as in part, on the radio; it has been anthologized in several important collections of verse; and has been cited by an increasing number of critics as a major nineteenth-century poem. Our edition restored the poem to its form before Clare's publisher, John Taylor, cut it about, or Clare himself tidied it up to meet his publishers' criticisms. We put back Clare's own punctuation (or the lack of it), we allowed his own spellings to stand (except in a very few instances), we restored his grammar, his vocabulary, his sensuality, and consequently his vigour. We allowed Clare to speak for himself. In these decisions we have been supported by John Barrell, who has written some of the best criticisms of Clare as a poet,[2] on the grounds that Clare's poetic vision required 'localness' of language

[1] M. Storey, *The Poetry of John Clare* (London: Macmillan, 1974), 25.

[2] See particularly, J. Barrell, *The Idea of Landscape and the Sense of Place: an Approach to the Poetry of John Clare* (Cambridge University Press, 1972) and *Poetry, Language and Politics* (Manchester University Press, 1988).

and form, and had quite different characteristics from the landscape poetry that preceded it. Clare has won a place in Poets' Corner, Westminster Abbey, and critics do not apologize for using the word 'great' when describing his status as a poet. More has been learnt about changes in early nineteenth-century language and the social structure that produced it, and readers today find fewer difficulties in reading Clare with the 'warts' (as many used to regard them) left in. Our knowledge of Clare's manuscripts has improved over the last thirty years and we can now present a much improved text for 1993, the bicentenary of Clare's birth.

The genesis of *The Shepherd's Calendar* was not easy. John Taylor changed his mind several times about what he wanted. In particular he turned away from a structure in which a descriptive poem for each month of the year was to be accompanied by a suitable verse-tale to the publication of a book significantly entitled *The Shepherd's Calendar, with Village Stories, and other Poems* (1827). This separating-out of some of the verse-tales, and the rejection of others, offended Clare's own judgement greatly, and we have sought to remedy the deficiency by publishing *Clare's Cottage Tales* (Carcanet Press, Manchester, 1993), because it is not possible to reconstruct the first intentions for the poem. Clare himself was relieved to see the book published at all. It had taken about six years to come to fruition and Clare had begun to think that it would never appear.

INTRODUCTION

But what sort of poem is it? If it is, in Storey's words, 'Clare's idea of the true pastoral', then it has to be admitted that its eventual form was a compromise, largely imposed by a publisher and editor who, in his ill-health and in a changing publishing climate, simply wanted to get the poem out. A publisher, moreover, who had frequently complained about Clare's descriptive realism and who had urged the poet to 'raise your Views generally, and speak of the Appearances of Nature each Month more philosophically (if I may say so) or with more Excitement ...' One does not know whether he wanted something more like Thomson's *Seasons*, with an argument prefacing each section of the poem elaborating upon the relationship of God, Man, and Nature, or whether he wanted a sort of spiritual autobiography in verse such as might have been expected from Wordsworth. Either of these possibilities would have produced a more 'philosophical' approach, but what can he have meant by 'more Excitement'? To the modern reader *The Shepherd's Calendar* is full of excitement and particularly so because of the accuracy of its portrayal of natural life in the different months of the the year. Such touches as:

> In the barn hole sits the cat
> Watching within the thirsty rat
> Who oft at morn its dwelling leaves
> To drink the moisture from the eaves
>
> ('September')

and:

The breeze is stopt the lazy bough
Hath not a leaf that dances now
The totter grass upon the hill
And spiders threads is hanging still
The feathers dropt from morehens wings
Which to the waters surface clings
As stedfast and as heavy seem
As stones beneath them in the stream
Hawkweed and groundsels fairey downs
Unruffld keep their seeding crowns
And in the oven heated air
Not one light thing is floating there

('July')

may not be philosophical but it is hard to deny
excitement to such vivid evocations of natural life.

Clare's muse is essentially popular, deriving much
strength from ballad and folk-song. Its language is full of
the liveliness of country speech and, above all, English,
despite the fact that he occasionally wrote poems in Scots
dialect. Its rootedness in popular culture can be seen in
the many references to *Old Moore's Almanac* and
Thomas Tusser's *Five Hundred Points of Good
Husbandry*. *The Shepherd's Calendar* itself is a species of
almanac. It relates the tasks to be performed in
agriculture in each month of the year: ploughing in
February, lambing in March, weeding in May, haymaking
in June, and so on. It describes the flowers, the birds, and
the beasts to be found in hedgerow and field. It
celebrates the festivals of the year: May Day games,
sheep-shearing feasts, Harvest Home, and Christmas.
And in general, it catalogues all the important occasions

to be met with in the farmer's year. In these characteristics it relates to such books as William Hone's *Everyday Book* or, a similar publication, *Time's Telescope*, a rather ambitious almanac to which Clare himself submitted poetry. When John Taylor suggested the idea of *The Shepherd's Calendar* he had in mind a long history of such books going back to the medieval period, with which he knew Clare was familiar. Almanacs were of different sorts, catering to different customers at different prices. Some were cheap and sold by every pedlar, such as *Old Moore's Almanac*; others were up-market like *Time's Telescope*, appealing to the literary middle-class. Some were devoted to a neighbourhood, naming the local fairs and markets in quite a small circuit; others were directed to a national market and acted as a kind of encyclopaedia. But all of them were geared to the essentially rural life of the great majority of British citizens. Clare's *Shepherd's Calendar* has an appeal to anyone who knows anything about nature in Britain or about farming life. It would have seemed a familiar genre to the ordinary reader in nineteenth-century Britain.

But it also reflects the nostalgia felt in a nation when agriculture was losing its pre-eminence and where industry and commerce were beginning to take over. The poem regrets the passing of the fairy-tale:

> Ah where is page of poesy
> So sweet as theirs was wont to be
> The majic wonders that decievd
> When fictions were as truths believd
>
> ('January: a Cottage Evening')

the songs and jokes:

> There they wi scraps of songs and laugh and tale
> Lighten their anual toils while merry ale
> Goes round and gladdens old mens hearts to praise
> The thread bare customs of old farmers days
>
> ('June')

the 'custom kiss', the May Day games, and the Christmas morris dancers. *The Shepherd's Calendar* regrets the passing of old customs, not only in the single individual life as childhood retreats, but also in society as a whole, as it too loses its innocence. We are said to be in the midst of a mood of nostalgia for our own rural past. If that is so, Clare cannot help but appeal to us. But in order to regret something that has been lost, we have to possess a keen imaginative awareness of it before we lost it. *The Shepherd's Calendar* provides this for us better than any other poem in the English language. As a poem it has the same luminous quality as Palmer's landscapes. And Clare's sense of loss is more than nostalgia because it is based on an awareness of what Clare's region was like before the onset of enclosure. For Clare, enclosure meant the loss of freedom to wander unimpeded across the fenlands, heath, and marsh, because his walks were interrupted by the fences of ownership and 'No Trespass' signs. In Taylor's version of 'June' the last four lines were omitted:

> As proud distinction makes a wider space
> Between the genteel and the vulgar race

> Then must they fade as pride oer custom showers
> Its blighting mildew on her feeble flowers

Taylor's treatment of Clare's poetry is like an encloser destroying local custom. Taylor changes many of Clare's 'provincialisms': 'burring' becomes 'buzzing', 'childern' becomes 'children', 'sturt' becomes 'steep', and so on. The syntax is smoothed out wherever possible. The local names are omitted if they offend Evangelical prudery. Thus the following lines were dropped from 'May':

> And smell smocks that from view retires
> Mong rustling leaves and bowing briars

and fairies no longer crowded in cupboards 'As thick as mites in rotten cheese'. The image was probably too strong for Taylor's 'cockney' customers. Sexuality is diminished. In Taylor's version, the labourer, 'stript in his shirt', is not allowed to sit beside the maiden 'in her unpind gown'. Once we read Clare as he wrote, with all his lively sensuality, we will never wish to return to Taylor's bowdlerized version. In Clare's eyes, however, Taylor was a representative of the classes with power in society, whom he must please if he was to succeed at all.

Fortunately, however, Taylor's view of pastoral poetry did not demand a plethora of dryads and fauns, nor a cast of aristocratic shepherds and shepherdesses. He may well have read John Gay's 'The Shepherd's Week' (1714), since an edition of Gay's poems appeared in 1795:

Thou wilt not find my Shepherdesses idly piping on oaten Reeds, but milking the Kine, tying up the Sheaves, or if the Hogs are astray driving them to their Styes. My Shepherd gathereth none other Nosegays but what are the growth of our own Fields, he sleepeth not under Myrtle shades, but under a Hedge, nor doth he vigilantly defend his Flocks from Wolves, because there are none ... [3]

As Clare said of Shenstone's pastorals, more was involved than 'Putting the Correct Language of the Gentleman into the Mouth of a Simple Shepherd or Vulgar Ploughman', but Taylor did at least recognize that an English pastoral did not have to be stuffed with Greek mythology. Clare thought of himself as belonging to a tradition of English pastoral that went as far back as Chaucer. The tradition contained within it such poems as Chaucer's 'Reeve's Tale', Herrick's 'The Horkey' and Gay's 'The Shepherd's Week', though the latter is ironic in its treatment of country lore where Clare is basically serious. Not that he could not be mocking of rural materialism in matters of courtship and marriage when he chose to be. In any event the romantic character of Clare's pastoral is often kept in check by a strong proverbial element:

> She shrinks away and blushing calls it rude
> But turns to smile and hopes to be pursued
>
> ('June')

or:

> While old dames say the sign is plain
> That she will dream about her swain

[3] *Scolar Press Facsimile*, 1969.

And toss the cloaths from off her bed
And cautions her of roguish ned
Holding their hands agen their hips
To laugh as up she starts and trips
In quickend speed along the town
Bidding good night to passing clown

('July')

Though Clare always spoke of Thomson's *Seasons* with respect almost amounting to awe, *The Shepherd's Calendar* is a very different poem from it. It was Bloomfield who was for Clare the greatest writer of pastorals in the English language. Barrell's comment on *The Seasons* is helpful:

In *The Seasons*, descriptions of landscape, which represent the social as well as the natural world as providentially ordered and perfectly harmonious, repeatedly give way, and on occasion within a single paragraph, to exhortations to more virtue, which represent society as corrupt and in urgent need of reformation. [4]

It is not that Clare's poem does not reflect upon the relationship between the landscape and social order but that Clare's viewpoint is, so to speak, on the flat while Thomson's is from the height. Thomson looks down and over the landscape: Clare is lost in it. Clare can describe workers in the field, the alternations of storm and sunshine, even expressions of simple Christian kindness, but he has no stomach for sermons on patriotism and industry. Thomson looks down upon the workers in the field: Clare struggles alongside them.

[4] Barrell, *Poetry, Language and Politics*, 93.

Yet, it is true to say of both poets, that their Nature is full of working agriculturalists, and the same may be said of Cowper's longer poems. Clare draws from such writers what he needs but always makes something new of it. It is, of course, an error to think of Clare as an unlettered man who wrote only from direct observation. Often, as he sat in the fields, he was frequently reading a book.

A calendar measures time and Clare's sense of time is highly developed, whether it be time of day, time of night, time of the week, month, or year, or the time of changing seasons. Even of historical time Clare has a vivid sense as when he writes of the daisy blossoming in Paradise and being trodden down by Adam and Eve. As far as the time of day goes, *The Shepherd's Calendar* is filled with references to altering shadows, homemade sun-clocks and the worker's observation of the height of the sun in the heavens. This does not prevent Clare from referring to mechanical time—the chiming of bells or the altering position of hands on the clock's dial. A labouring weeder, struggling with an arduous or boring task, is always asking the time of day, as the historian G. C. Coulton once perceptively observed. To the working man, too, the time of the week is also important. What evening is to the day, Sunday is to the week—rest after gruelling labour. Then there is Christmas, Clare tells us, the week with *two* Sundays. The year is thus punctuated by feast-days and holidays, or a welcome day of rain when outdoor work cannot be undertaken. *The Shepherd's Calendar* tells us more than any poem in the English language what time means to the working man, an experience that is being lost to us in our industrialized society. If we are to appreciate leisure, then we must endure labour. A new sense of time, taken from the factory clock, was beginning to permeate agriculture in Clare's day and he was aware of it. But what concerns him most is time as rhythm, as succession, as waves breaking upon a shore, as growth and decay, as birth, copulation, and death. And if he is a poet of Time, he is also a poet of Eternity. The Garden of Eden and Noah's Ark are meaningful to him, but so also are Creation and the Day of Judgement.

Clare's *Shepherd's Calendar* was more than Taylor understood. The publisher, for example, rejected 'July' out of hand and obliged Clare to write a second version, printed at the back of this volume. Yet the first version of 'July' is a good example of Clare's sense of simultaneity. The poem is first of all thronged with sexual reference—the lissom shapes of the raking girls beneath their cotton dresses, the 'smutty song and story gay', the labourers' rude jokes, the boy courting his girl by keeping her horn filled with ale and her pinafore with ripe fruit, or getting faggots of wood down from the pile on Sunday to save her church-going dress, the maid drawing cool water at the well for the passing boy, the May-game forfeits of kisses, the 'crumpling creases in her gown', and 'the whispering sweethearts chatting on'. This really is a hot day in July. It is also a day of hard sweating toil:

> Boys loading on the waggon stand
> And men below wi sturdy hand
> Heave up the shocks on lathy prong
> While horse boys lead the team along;

the boy bustles to and fro with food and drink; the gipsy cuts his bullrushes; the Scots drover drives his cattle by; the thresher, the blacksmith, the gardener, the cobbler, and the tailor are all hard at work. Even the birds, the insects and the animals share in the same tumult. Nowhere else in English poetry can such a full Breughelesque picture be found. Each vignette is startlingly precise but the total picture is almost exhausting in its plenitude.

Village superstitions, village gossip, village games are all reflected in the poem. Even a minor character in the broad scene is brought to life:

> The kitchen wench wi face red hot
> As blazing fire neath the supper pot
> Hath cleand her pails and pansions all
> And set them leaning by the wall

The chasing dog contrasts with the stillness of the air: the Scots drovers,

> so oddly clad
> In petticoats of banded plad
> Wi blankets oer their shoulders slung
> To camp at night the fields among
> When they for rest on commons stop
> And blue cap like a stocking top
> Cockt oer their faces summer brown
> Wi scarlet tazzeles on the crown

All have a Shakespearian verisimilitude.

Even so, we are never far from the concept of the homely almanac. 'November' is a case in point. A common feature of such booklets was a section on weather signs. Poems on this subject by Erasmus Darwin and Edward Jenner are frequently found in almanacs of the period. Lines on the subject also feature in John Gay's pastorals.[5] Clare takes such a commonplace and turns it, in 'November', into one of the liveliest poems in the whole volume. If the November weather is dull, the poem is not. The language is vigorous throughout and challenges attention. Compared with Gay, or Jenner, or Darwin, Clare's treatment of this familiar topic, though it employs many of the same facts, is in a creative order far superior to theirs. The 9-line stanza seems splendidly appropriate to this material because of the strength of the final longer line in each stanza. I recommend *The Shepherd's Calendar* to you, not only as the best almanac ever created, but as 'the truest poem of English country life ever written'.

E. R.

[5] Gay, 'The Shepherd's Week', *Scolar Press Facsimile*, 4–5, 11, 23–34.

NOTE ON THE TEXT

THIS new edition has been occasioned by the discovery
of errors during the, almost, quarter of a century since
this book was first brought out by Robinson and
Summerfield. Most of them consist of one-word mis-
readings but there are two places where the changes
are major: first, in 'July', where twenty-four lines have
been found to belong to another poem, 'A Sunday with
Shepherds and Herd Boys', which was composed at the
same period as 'July' and deals with closely connected
themes: and second, in 'October'. When Robinson
and Summerfield first read extensive handwritten
alterations to a draft of 'October', they concluded
that they were in the hand of John Taylor, Clare's
publisher, and therefore excluded them from the
1964 edition. Strangely enough, Clare's hand, when
he was writing very neatly, closely resembled
Taylor's. For reasons that will be given in more detail
in our OET *Collected Poems of John Clare*, we have
decided that the alterations to 'October' should be
restored and the poem reordered so that it is now
much closer to the poem as it was when first published. There is good reason to believe that all of
Clare's manuscripts for *The Shepherd's Calendar*
have not survived and it may well be that Clare
amended 'October' in accordance with suggestions
made to him by Taylor. Comparison between the
present edition and the 1964 edition will show in

'October' significant changes in tone that require further study.

When Taylor first published *The Shepherd's Calendar* in 1827 he made considerable alterations to Clare's manuscripts, acknowledging to the poet that he had 'been compelled to cut out a vast many lines'. For example, he compelled Clare to rewrite 'July' completely. As in 1964, we have returned to Clare's first version and print the second version at the end of the other poems. Taylor said of 'July': 'Instead of cutting out of the poem on July what is bad, I am obliged to look earnestly to find anything that is good.' The reader will judge for herself or himself, but we totally disagree with Clare's publisher and think that 'July' is a poem of a very high order. Taylor also bowdlerized Clare, omitting passages that were rich with rustic sensuality. He censored Clare's language and sometimes omitted Clare's political comments. A lively debate has arisen about Taylor's editorship of Clare, but Clare once said 'Editors are troubled with nice amendings & if Doctors were as fond of amputation as they are of altering & correcting the world would have nothing but cripples.' Considering the number of amputations in Clare's day, this is no small criticism. Taylor tidied up Clare's grammar and corrected his punctuation and spelling. All these emendations robbed Clare's work of much of the particularity and locality of language that are among the poet's greatest strengths.

Since this is an edition for the general reader, we

have made some minimal alterations. We have replaced ampersands by 'ands'. We have silently substituted 'where' for 'were' throughout where the sense demanded it, 'there' for 'their' and vice versa, and 'ne'er' for 'neer' and 'near'. We have also punctuated 'hell', 'shell', and 'Ill' to 'he'll', 'she'll', and 'I'll' to make the reader's task easier. At one point we have printed 'while' for 'whiele' and we have changed 'eves' to eaves' when necessary. (Here and there 'eves' and 'eaves' occur quite close together in the text.) Clare tends to divide his words in such a way that the meaning is underlined: 'hous wife' for 'housewife', 'key holes' for 'keyholes' and 'wood' land for 'woodland'. We have preserved this habit. But we have substituted 'cotes' for 'coats' and 'whey' for 'way' to save the reader trouble. We have silently supplied missing letters or syllables where the sense unmistakably demanded them. It is quite impossible to distinguish in Clare's manuscripts between 'ing' and 'y' at the end of a word, so that here and there we have changed our minds since 1964, preferring, for example, 'hidy holes' to 'hiding holes' because the former is part of the English vernacular. We maintain, however, that these alterations are minimal in comparison with those made by earlier editors and that the original flavour of Clare's language has been preserved. We are more conservative still in our OET edition.

Glossary and notes have been combined at the back of the book except when it seemed important to place a comment on the page of the text so that the reader might not be held up. Full discussion of our editorial methods is reserved for the OET volumes. The manuscripts used are mostly from the Peterborough Museum, to whose curators and attendants we owe a special debt.

JANUARY

A WINTERS DAY

Withering and keen the winter comes
While confort flyes to close shut rooms
And sees the snow in feathers pass
Winnowing by the window glass
And unfelt tempests howl and beat   5
Above his head in corner seat
And musing oer the changing scene
Farmers behind the tavern screne
Sit—or wi elbow idly prest
On hob reclines the corners guest   10

Reading the news to mark again
The bankrupt lists or price of grain
Or old moores anual prophecys
That many a theme for talk supplys
Whose almanacks thumbd pages swarm   15
Wi frost and snow and many a storm
And wisdom gossipd from the stars
Of politics and bloody wars
He shakes his head and still proceeds
Ne'er doubting once of what he reads   20
All wonders are wi faith supplyd
Bible at once and weather guide
Puffing the while his red tipt pipe
Dreaming oer troubles nearly ripe
Yet not quite lost in profits way   25
He'll turn to next years harvest day
And winters leisure to regale
Hopes better times and sips his ale
While labour still pursues his way
And braves the tempest as he may   30
The thresher first thro darkness deep
Awakes the mornings winter sleep
Scaring the owlet from her prey
Long before she dreams of day
That blinks above head on the snow   35
Watching the mice that squeaks below
And foddering boys sojourn again
By ryhme¹ hung hedge and frozen plain
Shuffling thro the sinking snows
Blowing his fingers as he goes   40

¹ = rime.

2

To where the stock in bellowings hoarse
Call for their meals in dreary close
And print full many a hungry track
Round circling hedge that guards the stack
Wi higgling tug he cuts the hay   45
And bares the forkfull loads away
And morn and evening daily throws
The little heaps upon the snows
The shepherd too in great coat wrapt
And straw bands round his stockings lapt   50
Wi plodding dog that sheltering steals
To shun the wind behind his heels
Takes rough and smooth the winter weather
And paces thro the snow together
While in the fields the lonly plough   55
Enjoys its frozen sabbath now
And horses too pass time away
In leisures hungry holiday
Rubbing and lunging round the yard
Dreaming no doubt of summer sward   60
As near wi idle pace they draw
To brouze the upheapd cribs of straw
While whining hogs wi hungry roar
Crowd around the kitchen door
Or when their scanty meal is done   65
Creep in the straw the cold to shun
And old hens scratting all the day
Seeks curnels chance may throw away
Pausing to pick the seed and grain
Then dusting up the chaff again   70

3

While in the barn holes hid from view
The cats their patient watch pursue
For birds which want in flocks will draw
From woods and fields to pick the straw
The soodling boy that saunters round   75
The yard on homward dutys bound
Now fills the troughs for noisy hogs
Oft asking aid from barking dogs
That tuggles at each flopping ear
Of such as scramble on too near   80
Or circld round wi thirsty stock
That for his swinging labours flock
At clanking pump his station takes
Half hid in mist their breathing makes
Or at the pond before the door   85
Which every night leaves frozen ocr
Wi heavy beetle[1] splinters round
The glossy ice wi jarring sound
While huddling geese as half asleep
Doth round the imprisond water creep   90
Silent and sad to wait his aid
And soon as ere a hole is made
They din his ears wi pleasures cry
And hiss at all that ventures nigh
Splashing wi jealous joys and vain   95
Their fill ere it be froze again
And woodstack climbs at maids desire
Throwing down faggots for the fire
Where stealing time he often stands
To warm his half froze tingling hands   100

[1] See Glossary

The schoolboy still in dithering joys
Pastime in leisure hours employs
And be the weather as it may
Is never at a loss for play
Rolling up jiant heaps of snow   105
As noontide frets its little thaw
Making rude things of various names
Snow men or aught their fancy frames
Till numbd wi cold they quake away
And join at hotter sports to play   110
Kicking wi many a flying bound
The foot ball oer the frozen ground
Or seeking bright glib ice to play
To sailing slide the hours away
As smooth and quick as shadows run   115
When clouds in autumn pass the sun
Some hurrying rambles eager take
To skait upon the meadow lake
Scaring the snipe from her retreat
From shelving banks unfrozen seat   120
Or running brook where icy spars
Which the pale sunlight specks wi stars
Shoots crizzling oer the restless tide
To many a likness petrified
Where fancy often stoops to pore   125
And turns again to wonder more
The more hen too wi fear opprest
Starts from her reedy shelterd nest
Bustling to get from foes away
And scarcly flies more fast then they   130

5

Skaiting along wi curving springs
Wi arms spread out like herons wings
They race away for pleasures sake
A hunters speed along the lake
And oft neath trees where ice is thin   135
Meet narrow scapes from breaking in
Again the robin waxes tame
And ventures pitys crumbs to claim
Picking the trifles off the snow
Which dames on purpose daily throw   140
And perching on the window sill
Where memory recolecting still
Knows the last winters broken pane
And there he hops and peeps again
The clouds of starnels dailey fly   145
Blackening thro the evening sky
To whittleseas[1] reed wooded mere
And ozier holts by rivers near
And many a mingld swathy crowd
Rook crow and jackdaw noising loud   150
Fly too and fro to dreary fen
Dull winters weary flight agen
Flopping on heavy wings away
As soon as morning wakens grey
And when the sun sets round and red   155
Returns to naked woods to bed
Wood pigeons too in flocks appear
By hunger tamd from timid fear

[1] Whittlesea, Cambridgeshire. For a map which clearly indicates the extent of this mere, see H. C. Darby, *The Draining of the Fens*, Cambridge, 1956, p. 230.

They mid the sheep unstartld steal
And share wi them a scanty meal   160
Picking the green leaves want bestows
Of turnips sprouting thro the snows
The ickles from the cottage eaves
Which cold nights freakish labour leaves
Fret in the sun a partial thaw   165
Pattring on the pitted snow
The sun soon creepeth out of sight
Behind the woods—and running night
Makes haste to shut the days dull eye
And grizzles oer the chilly sky   170
Dark deep and thick by day forsook
As cottage chimneys sooty nook
While maidens fresh as summer roses
Joining from the distant closes
Haste home wi yokes and swinging pail   175
And thresher too sets by his flail
And leaves the mice at peace again
To fill their holes wi stolen grain
And owlets glad his toils are oer
Swoops by him as he shuts the door   180
The shepherd seeks his cottage warm
And tucks his hook beneath his arm
And weary in the cold to roam
Scenting the track that leadeth home
His dog wi swifter pace proceeds   185
And barks to urge his masters speed
Then turns and looks him in the face
And trotts before wi mending pace

7

Till out of whistle from the swain
He sits him down and barks again   190
Anxious to greet the opend door
And meet the cottage fire once more
The robin that wi nimble eye
Glegs round a danger to espy
Now pops from out the opend door   195
From crumbs half left upon the floor
Nor wipes his bill on perching chair
Nor stays to clean a feather there
Scard at the cat that sliveth in
A chance from evenings glooms to win   200
To jump on chairs or tables nigh
Seeking what plunder may supply
The childerns litterd scraps to thieve
Or aught that negligence may leave
Creeping when huswives cease to watch   205
Or dairey doors are off the latch
On cheese or butter to regale
Or new milk reeking in the pale
The hedger now in leather coat
From wood land wilds and fields remote   210
After a journey far and slow
Knocks from his shoes the caking snow
And opes the welcome creaking door
Throwing his faggot on the floor
And at his listning wifes desire   215
To eke afresh the blazing fire
Wi sharp bill cuts the hazel bands
Then sets him down to warm his hands

And tell in labours happy way
His story of the passing day   220
While as the warm blaze cracks and gleams
The supper reeks in savoury steams
Or keetle simmers merrily
And tinkling cups are set for tea
Thus doth the winters dreary day   225
From morn to evening wear away

JANUARY

A COTTAGE EVENING

The shutters closd the lamp alight
The faggot chopt and blazing bright
The shepherd from his labour free
Dancing his childern on his knee
Or toasting sloe boughs sputtering ripe   5
Or smoaking glad his puthering pipe
While underneath his masters seat
The tird dog lies in slumbers sweet
Startling and whimpering in his sleep
Chasing still the straying sheep   10
The cat rolld round in vacant chair
Or leaping childerns knees to lair
Or purring on the warmer hearth
Sweet chorus to the crickets mirth
The red cap hanging over head   15
In cage of wire is perchd abed
Slumbering in his painted feathers
Unconcous of the outdoor weathers
And things wi out the cottage walls
Meet comfort as the evening falls   20
As happy in the winters dearth
As those around the blazing hearth

The ass frost drove from off the moors
Where storms thro naked bushes roars
And not a leaf or sprig of green   25
On ground or quaking bush is seen
Save grey veind ivys hardy pride
Round old trees by the common side
Litterd wi straw now dozes warm
Neath the yard hovel from the storm   30
The swine well fed and in the sty
And fowl snug perchd in hovel nigh
Wi head in feathers safe asleep
Where fox finds ne'er a hole to creep
And geese that gabble in their dreams   35
Of litterd corn and thawing streams
The sparrow too their daily guest
Is in the cottage eaves at rest
And robin small and smaller wren
Are in their warm holes safe agen   40
From falling snows that winnow bye
The hovels where they nightly lye
And ague winds that shake the tree
Where other birds are forcd to be
The hus wife busy night and day   45
Cleareth the supper things away
While jumping cat starts from her seat
And streaking up on weary feet
The dog wakes at the welcome tones
That calls him up to pick the bones   50
On corner walls a glittering row
Hang fire irons less for use then show

11

Tongues bright wi hus wifes rubbing toil
Whod sooner burn her hands then soil
When sticks want mending up and when   55
Mores sought to eke the blaze agen
And sifter[1] dengling by their side
And poker in the fire untryd
And horshoe brightend as a spell
Witchcrafts evil powers to quell   60
And warming pan reflecting bright
The crackling blazes twittering light
That hangs the corner wall to grace
And seldom taken from its place
Save when the winter keener falls   65
Searching thro the cottage walls
Then quaking from the cottage fire
Warm beds as comforts they require
Yet still tis bright as gold can be
And childern often peep to see   70
Their laughing faces as they pass
Gleam on the lid as plain as glass
Things cleard away then down she sits
And tells her tales by starts and fits
Not willing to loose time or toil   75
She knits or sues[2] and talks the while
Somthing as may be warnings found
To the young listners gaping round
Of boys who in her early day
Strolld to the meadow lake to play   80
And skaited races void of fear
Oer deeps or shallows any where

---

[1] See Glossary.   [2] = sews.

12

Till willows oer the brink inclind
Shelterd the water from the wind
And left it scarcly crizzld oer   85
When one plopt in to rise no more
And how upon a market night
When ne'er a star bestowd its light
A farmers shepherd oer his glass
Forgot that he had woods to pass   90
Who overtook by darkness deep
Had been to sell his masters sheep
Till coming wi his startld horse
To where two roads a hollow cross
Where lone guide when a stranger strays   95
A white post points four different ways
There by the woodsides lonly gate
A murdering robber lay in wait
The frighted horse wi broken rein
Stood at the stable door again   100
But none came home to fill his rack
Or take the saddle from his back
The saddle it was all he bore
The man was seen alive no more
In her young days beside the wood   105
The gibbet in its terror stood
Tho now all gone tis not forgot
Still dreaded as a haunted spot
And from her memory oft repeats
Witches dread powers and fairey feats   110
How one has oft been known to prance
In cowcribs like a coach to france

And rid[1] on sheep trays from the fold
A race horse speed to burton hold[2]
To join the midnight mysterys rout   115
Where witches meet the yews about
And how when met wi unawares
They instant turn to cats or hares
And race along wi hellish flight
Now here and there and out of sight   120
And how the tother tiny things
Will leave their moonlight meadow rings
And unpercievd thro keyholes creep
When alls in bed and fast asleep
And crowd in cupboards as they please   125
As thick as mites in rotten cheese
To feast on what the cotter leaves
For mice ant[3] reckond bigger thieves
They take away too well as[4] eat
And still the hus wifes eye they cheat   130
Nothing to miss as other thieves
Alls left the same as she percieves
In spite of all the crowds that swarm
In cottage small and larger farm
That thro each key hole pop and pop   135
Like wasps into a grocers shop
Wi all the things that they can win
From chance to put their plunders in

---

[1] = rode.
[2] Burton Hold = Burton Old or Burton Wold. See A. Mawer and F. M. Stenton, *The Place Names of Northamptonshire*, 1933, p. 180.
[3] See Glossary.   [4] = as well as.

14

The shells of wallnuts split in two
By crows who wi the curnels flew   140
And acorn cups by stock doves pluckt
And eggshells by a cuckoo suckt
That hold what ever things they please
Stole tea or sugar bread or cheese
Wi broad leaves of the sycamore   145
To rap¹ as cloths their daintys oer
And hazel nutts when they regale
In cellars brought to hold their ale
Wi bungholes squirrels bored well
To get the curnel from the shell   150
Or maggots a way out to win
When all was eat that grew within
And be the key holes ere so high
Rush poles a laders help supply
Where soft the climbers fearless tread   155
On spindles made of bentv thread
And foul or fair or dark the night
Their wild fire lamps are ready light
For which full many a daring crime
Is acted in the summer time   160
When glowworms found in lanes remote
Is murderd for its shining coat
And put in flowers that nature weaves
Wi hollow shapes and silken leaves
Such as the canterbury bell   165
Serving for lamp or lanthorn well
Or following wi unwearied watch
The flight of one they cannot match

¹ = wrap.

15

As silence sliveth upon sleep
Or thieves by dozing watchdogs creep   170
They steal from Jack a lanthorns tails
A light whose guidance never fails
To aid them in the darkest night
And guide their plundering steps aright
Rattling away in printless tracks   175
Some horsd on beetles glossy backs
Go wisking on and others hie
As fast as loaded moths can flye
Some urge the morning cock to shun
The hardest gallop mice can run   180
In chariots lolling at their ease
Made of what ere their fancys please
Things that in childhoods memory dwells
Scoopd crow-pot-stones or cockle shells
Wi weels at hand of mallow seeds   185
Where childish sports were stringing beads
And thus equipd they softly pass
Like shadows on the summer grass
And drive away in troops together
Just as the spring wind drives a feather   190
They ride oer insects as a stone
Nor bruize a limb nor brake a bone
As light as happy dreams they creep
Nor brake the feeblest link of sleep
A midgeon in their road abed   195
Ne'er feels the wheels run oer his head
But sleeps till sunrise calls him up
Unconsous of the passing troop

Thus dames the winter night regales
Wi wonders never ceasing tales   200
While in the corner ill at ease
Or crushing tween their fathers knees
The childern silent all the while
And een repressd the laugh or smile
Quake wi the ague chills of fear   205
And tremble while they love to hear
Startling while they the tales recall
At their own shadows on the wall
Till the old clock that strikes unseen
Behind the picture pasted screene   210
Where Eve and Adam still agree
To rob lifes fatal apple tree
Counts over bed times hour of rest
And bids each be sleeps fearful guest
She then her half told tales will leave   215
To finish on tomorrows eve
The childern cringe away to bed
And up the ladder softly tread
Scarce daring from their fearful joys
To look behind or make a noise   220
Nor speak a word but still as sleep
They secret to their pillows creep
And whisper oer in terrors way
The prayers they dare no louder say
And hide their heads beneath the cloaths   225
And try in vain to seek repose
While yet to fancys sleepless eye
Witches on sheep trays gallop bye

17

And faireys like to rising sparks
Swarm twittering round them in the dark   230
Till sleep creeps nigh to ease their cares
And drops upon them unawares
O spirit of the days gone bye
Sweet childhoods fearful extacy
The witching spells of winter nights   235
Where are they fled wi their delights
When listning on the corner seat
The winter evenings length to cheat
I heard my mothers memory tell
Tales superstition loves so well   240
Things said or sung a thousand times
In simple prose or simpler ryhmes
Ah where is page of poesy
So sweet as theirs was wont to be
The majic wonders that decievd   245
When fictions were as truths believd
The fairey feats that once prevaild
Told to delight and never faild
Where are they now their fears and sighs
And tears from founts of happy eyes   250
Breathless suspense and all their crew
To what wild dwelling have they flew
I read in books but find them not
For poesy hath its youth forgot
I hear them told to childern still   255
But fear ne'er numbs my spirits chill
I still see faces pale wi dread
While mine coud laugh at what is said

18

See tears imagind woes supply
While mine wi real cares are dry   260
Where are they gone the joys and fears
The links the life of other years
I thought they bound around my heart
So close that we coud never part
Till reason like a winters day   265
Nipt childhoods visions all away
Nor left behind one withering flower
To cherish in a lonly hour
Memory may yet the themes repeat
But childhoods heart doth cease to beat   270
At storys reasons sterner lore
Turneth like gossips from her door
The majic fountain where the head
Rose up just as the startld maid
Was stooping from the weedy brink   275
To dip her pitcher in to drink
That did its half hid mystery tell
To smooth its hair and use it well
Who doing as it bade her do
Turnd to a king and lover too   280
The tale of Cinderella told
The winter thro and never old
The faireys favourite and friend
Who made her happy in the end
The pumpkin that at her approach   285
Was turnd into a golden coach
The rats that faireys majic knew
And instantly to horses grew

And coachmen ready at her call
To drive her to the princes ball   290
With fur changd jackets silver lind
And tails hung neath their hats behind
Where soon as met the princes sight
She made his heart ach all the night
The golden glove wi fingers small   295
She lost while dancing in the hall
That was on every finger tryd
And fitted hers and none beside
When cinderella soon as seen
Was woo'd and won and made a queen   300
The boy that did the jiants slay
And gave his mothers cows away
For majic mask that day or night
When on woud keep him out of sight
And running beans not such as weaves   305
Round poles the height of cottage eaves
But majic ones that travelld high
Some steeples journeys up the sky
And reachd a jiants dwelling there
A cloud built castle in the air   310
Where venturing up the fearfull height
That servd him climbing half the night
He searchd the jiants coffers oer
And never wanted wealth no more
While like a lion scenting food   315
The jiant roard in hungry mood
A storm of threats that might suffice
To freeze the hottest blood to ice

And make when heard however bold
The strongest heart strings cramp wi cold 320
But mine sleeps on thro fear and dread
And terrors that might wake the dead
When like a lion in the wood
He snufts and tracks the scent of blood
And vows if aught falls in his power 325
He'll grind their very bones to flower[1]
I hear it now nor dream of harm
The storm is settld to a calm
Those fears are dead what will not dye
In fading lifes mortality 330
Those truths are fled and left behind
A real world and doubting mind

[1] = flour.

FEBRUARY

A THAW

The snow is gone from cottage tops
The thatch moss glows in brighter green
And eaves in quick succession drops
Where grinning icicles hath been
Pit patting wi a pleasant noise   5
In tubs set by the cottage door
And ducks and geese wi happy joys
Douse in the yard pond brimming oer

The sun peeps thro the window pane
Which childern mark wi laughing eye   10
And in the wet street steal again
To tell each other spring is nigh
And as young hope the past recalls
In playing groups will often draw
Building beside the sunny walls   15
Their spring-play-huts of sticks or straw

And oft in pleasures dreams they hie
Round homsteads by the village side
Scratting the hedgrow mosses bye
Where painted pooty shells abide   20
Mistaking oft the ivy spray
For leaves that come wi budding spring
And wondering in their search for play
Why birds delay to build and sing

The milk maid singing leaves her bed   25
As glad as happy thoughts can be
While mag pies chatter oer her head
As jocund in the change as she
Her cows around the closes stray
Nor lingering wait the foddering boy   30
Tossing the molehills in their play
And staring round in frolic joy

Ploughmen go whistling to their toils
And yoke again the rested plough
And mingling oer the mellow soils   35
Boys shouts and whips are noising now

23

The shepherd now is often seen
By warm banks oer his hook to bend
Or oer a gate or stile to lean
Chattering to a passing friend   40

Odd hive bees fancying winter oer
And dreaming in their combs of spring
Creeps on the slab beside their door
And strokes its legs upon its wing
While wild ones half asleep are humming   45
Round snowdrop bells a feeble note
And pigions coo of summer coming
Picking their feathers on the cote

The barking dogs by lane and wood
Drive sheep afield from foddering ground   50
And eccho in her summer mood
Briskly mocks the cheery sound
The flocks as from a prison broke
Shake their wet fleeces in the sun
While following fast a misty smoke   55
Reeks from the moist grass as they run

Nor more behind his masters heels
The dog creeps oer his winter pace
But cocks his tail and oer the fields
Runs many a wild and random chase   60
Following in spite of chiding calls
The startld cat in harmless glee
Scaring her up the weed green walls
Or mossy mottld apple tree

As crows from morning perches flye   65
He barks and follows them in vain
Een larks will catch his nimble eye
And off he starts and barks again
Wi breathless haste and blinded guess
Oft following where the hare hath gone   70
Forgetting in his joys excess
His frolic puppy days are done

The gossips saunter in the sun
As at the spring from door to door
Of matters in the village done   75
And secret newsings mutterd oer
Young girls when they each other meet
Will stand their tales of love to tell
While going on errands down the street
Or fetching water from the well   80

A calm of pleasure listens round
And almost whispers winter bye
While fancy dreams of summer sounds
And quiet rapture fills the eye
The sun beams on the hedges lye   85
The south wind murmers summer soft
And maids hang out white cloaths to dry
Around the eldern skirted croft

Each barns green thatch reeks in the sun
Its mate the happy sparrow calls   90
And as nest building spring begun
Peeps in the holes about the walls

25

The wren a¹ sunny side the stack
Wi short tail ever on the strunt
Cockd gadding up above his back   95
Again for dancing gnats will hunt

The gladdend swine bolt from the sty
And round the yard in freedom run
Or stretching in their slumbers lye
Beside the cottage in the sun   100
The young horse whinneys to its mate
And sickens from the threshers door
Rubbing the straw yards banded gate
Longing for freedom on the moor

Hens leave their roosts wi cackling calls   105
To see the barn door free from snow
And cocks flye up the mossy walls
To clap their spangld wings and crow
About the steeples sunny top
The jackdaw flocks resemble spring   110
And in the stone archd windows pop
Wi summer noise and wanton wing

The small birds think their wants are oer
To see the snow hills fret again
And from the barns chaff litterd door   115
Betake them to the greening plain
The woodmans robin startles coy
Nor longer at his elbow comes
To peck wi hungers eager joy
Mong mossy stulps the litterd crumbs   120

¹ See Glossary.

Neath hedge and walls that screen the wind
The gnats for play will flock together
And een poor flyes odd hopes will find
To venture in the mocking weather
From out their hidy holes again   125
Wi feeble pace they often crecp
Along the sun warmd window pane
Like dreaming things that walk in sleep

The mavis thrush wi wild delight
Upon the orchards dripping tree   130
Mutters to see the day so bright
Spring scraps of young hopes poesy
And oft dame stops her burring wheel
To hear the robins note once more
That tutles while he pecks his meal   135
From sweet-briar hips beside the door

The hedghog from its hollow root
Sees the wood moss clear of snow
And hunts each hedge for fallen fruit
Crab hip and winter bitten sloe   140
And oft when checkd by sudden fears
As shepherd dog his haunt espies
He rolls up in a ball of spears
And all his barking rage defies

Thus nature of the spring will dream   145
While south winds thaw but soon again
Frost breaths upon the stiffening stream
And numbs it into ice—the plain

Soon wears its merry garb of white
And icicles that fret at noon   150
Will eke their icy tails at night
Beneath the chilly stars and moon

Nature soon sickens of her joys
And all is sad and dumb again
Save merry shouts of sliding boys   155
About the frozen furrowd plain
The foddering boy forgets his song
And silent goes wi folded arms
And croodling shepherds bend along
Crouching to the whizzing storms   160

MARCH

March month of 'many weathers' wildly comes
In hail and snow and rain and threatning hums
And floods: while often at his cottage door
The shepherd stands to hear the distant roar
Loosd from the rushing mills and river locks   5
Wi thundering sound and over powering shocks
And headlong hurry thro the meadow brigs
Brushing the leaning willows fingering twigs
In feathery foam and eddy hurryng chase
Rolling a storm oertaken travellers pace   10
From bank to bank along the meadow leas
Spreading and shining like to little seas

While in the pale sunlight a watery brood
Of swopping white birds flock about the flood
Yet winter seems half weary of its.toil   15
And round the ploughman on the elting soil
Will thread a minutes sun shine wild and warm
Thro the raggd places of the swimming storm
And oft the shepherd in his path will spye
The little daisey in the wet grass lye   20
That to the peeping sun enlivens gay
Like Labour smiling on an holiday
And where the stunt bank fronts the southern sky
By lanes or brooks where sunbeams love to lye
A cowslip peep will open faintly coy   25
Soon seen and gatherd by a wandering boy
A tale of spring around the distant haze
Seems muttering pleasures wi the lengthning days
Morn wakens mottld oft wi may day stains
And shower drops hang the grassy sprouting plains   30
And on the naked thorns of brassy hue
Drip glistning like a summer dream of dew
While from the hill side freshning forest drops
As one might walk upon their thickening tops
And buds wi young hopes promise seemly swells   35
Where woodman that in wild seclusion dwells
Wi chopping toil the coming spring decieves
Of many dancing shadows flowers and leaves
And in his pathway down the mossy wood
Crushes wi hasty feet full many a bud   40
Of early primrose yet if timely spied
Shelterd some old half rotten stump beside

The sight will cheer his solitery hour
And urge his feet to stride and save the flower
Muffld in baffles leathern coat and gloves   45
The hedger toils oft scaring rustling doves
From out the hedgrows who in hunger browze
The chockolate berrys on the ivy boughs
And flocking field fares speckld like the thrush
Picking the red awe from the sweeing bush   50
That come and go on winters chilly wing
And seem to share no sympethy wi spring
The stooping ditcher in the water stands
Letting the furrowd lakes from off the lands
Or splashing cleans the pasture brooks of mud   55
Where many a wild weed freshens into bud
And sprouting from the bottom purply green
The water cresses neath the wave is seen
Which the old woman gladly drags to land
Wi reaching long rake in her tottering hand   60
The ploughman mawls along the doughy sloughs
And often stop their songs to clean their ploughs
From teazing twitch that in the spongy soil
Clings round the colter terryfying toil
The sower striding oer his dirty way   65
Sinks anckle deep in pudgy sloughs and clay
And oer his heavy hopper stoutly leans
Strewing wi swinging arms the pattering beans
Which soon as aprils milder weather gleams
Will shoot up green between the furroed seams   70
The driving boy glad when his steps can trace
The swelling edding as a resting place

Slings from his clotted shoes the dirt around
And feign[1] woud rest him on the solid ground
And sings when he can meet the parting green   75
Of rushy balks that bend the lands between
While close behind em struts the nauntling crow
And daws whose heads seem powderd oer wi snow
To seek the worms—and rooks a noisey guest
That on the wind rockd elms prepares her nest   80
On the fresh furrow often drops to pull
The twitchy roots and gathering sticks and wool
Neath trees whose dead twigs litter to the wind
And gaps where stray sheep left their coats behind
While ground larks on a sweeing clump of rushes   85
Or on the top twigs of the oddling bushes
Chirp their 'cree creeing' note that sounds of spring
And sky larks meet the sun wi flittering wing
Soon as the morning opes its brightning eye
Large clouds of sturnels blacken thro the sky   90
From ozier holts about the rushy fen
And reed shaw borders by the river Nen
And wild geese regiments now agen repair
To the wet bosom of broad marshes there
In marching coloms and attention all   95
Listning and following their ring leaders call
The shepherd boy that hastens now and then
From hail and snow beneath his sheltering den
Of flags or file leavd sedges tyd in sheaves
Or stubble shocks oft as his eye percieves   100
Sun threads struck out wi momentary smiles
Wi fancy thoughts his lonliness beguiles

[1] = fain.

Thinking the struggling winter hourly bye
As down the edges of the distant sky
The hail storm sweeps—and while he stops to strip   105
The stooping hedgbriar of its lingcring hip
He hears the wild geese gabble oer his head
And pleasd wi fancys in his musings bred
He marks the figurd forms in which they flye
And pausing follows wi a wondering eye   110
Likening their curious march in curves or rows
To every letter which his memory knows
While far above the solitary crane
Swings lonly to unfrozen dykes again
Cranking a jarring mellancholy cry   115
Thro the wild journey of the cheerlcss sky
Full oft at early seasons mild and fair
March bids farewell wi garlands in her hair
Of hazel tassles woodbines hairy sprout
And sloe and wild plumb blossoms peeping out   120
In thick set knotts of flowers preparing gay
For aprils reign a mockery of may
That soon will glisten on the earnest eye
Like snow white cloaths hung in the sun to drye
The old dame often stills her burring wheel   125
When the bright sun will thro the window steal
And gleam upon her face and dancing fall
In diamond shadows on the picturd wall
While the white butterflye as in amaze
Will settle on the glossy glass to gaze   130
And oddling bee oft patting passing bye
As if they care to tell her spring was nigh

And smiling glad to see such things once more
Up she will get and potter to the door
And look upon the trees beneath the eaves   135
Sweet briar and ladslove swelling into leaves
And damsin trees thick notting into bloom
And goosberry blossoms on the bushes come
And stooping down oft views her garden beds
To see the spring flowers pricking out their heads   140
And from her apron strings she'll often pull
Her sissars out an early bunch to cull
For flower pots on the window board to stand
Where the old hour glass spins its thread of sand
And maids will often mark wi laughing eye   145
In elder where they hang their cloaths to drye
The sharp eyd robin hop from grain to grain
Singing its little summer notes again
As a sweet pledge of Spring the little lambs
Bleat in the varied weather round their dams   150
Or hugh molehill or roman mound behind
Like spots of snow lye shelterd from the wind
While the old yoes bold wi maternal cares
Looses their fears and every danger dares
Who if the shepherds dog but turns his eye   155
And stops behind a moment passing bye
Will stamp draw back and then their threats repeat
Urging defiance wi their stamping feet
And stung wi cares hopes cannot recconsile
They stamp and follow till he leaps a stile   160
Or skulking from their threats betakes to flight
And wi the master lessens out of sight

Clowns mark the threetning rage of march pass bye
And clouds wear thin and ragged in the sky
While wi less sudden and more lasting smiles   165
The growing sun their hopes of spring beguiles
Who often at its end remark wi pride
Days lengthen in their visits a 'cocks stride'
Dames clean their candlesticks and set them bye
Glad of the makeshift light that eves supply   170
The boy returning home at night from toil
Down lane and close oer footbrig gate and style[1]
Oft trembles into fear and stands to hark
The waking fox renew his short gruff bark
While badgers eccho their dread evening shrieks   175
And to his thrilling thoughts in terror speaks
And shepherds that wi in their hulks remain
Night after night upon the chilly plain
To watch the dropping lambs that at all hours
Come in the quaking blast like early flowers   180
Demanding all the shepherds care who find
Warm hedge side spots and take them from the wind
And round their necks in wary caution tyes
Long shreds of rags in red or purple dyes
Thats meant in danger as a safty spell   185
Like the old yoe that wears a tinkling bell
The sneaking foxes from his thefts to fright
That often seizes the young lambs at night
These when they in their nightly watchings hear
The badgers shrieks can hardly stifle fear   190
They list the noise from woodlands dark recess
Like helpless shrieking woman in distress

[1] = stile.

And oft as such fears fancying mistery
Believes the dismal yelling sounds to be
For superstition hath its thousand tales   195
To people all his midnight woods and vales
And the dread spot from whence the dismal noise
Mars the night musings of thcir dark employs
Owns its sad tale to realize their fear
At which their hearts in boyhood achd to hear   200
A maid at night by treacherous love decoyd
Was in that`shrieking wood years past destroyd
She went twas said to meet the waiting swain
And home and friends ne'er saw her face again
Mid brakes and thorns that crowded round the dell   205
And matting weeds that had no tongues to tell
He murderd her alone at dead midnight
While the pale moon threw round her sickly light
And loud shrieks left the thickets slumbers deep
That only scard the little birds from sleep   210
When the pale murdercrs terror frowning eye
Told its dread errand that the maid shoud dye
Mid thick black thorns her secret grave was made
And there wi night thc murderd girl was laid
When no one saw the deed but god and he   215
And moonlight sparkling thro the sleeping tree
Around—the red breast might at morning steel
There for the worm to meet his morning meal
In fresh turnd moulds that first beheld the sun
Nor knew the deed that dismal night had done   220
Such is the tale that superstition gives
And in her midnight memory ever lives

That makes the boy run by wi wild affright
And shepherds startle on their rounds at night

Now love teazd maidens from their droning wheels 225
At the red hour of sun set sliving steals
From scolding dames to meet their swains again
Tho water checks their visits oer the plain
They slive where no one sees some wall behind
Or orchard apple trees that stops the wind   230
To talk about springs pleasures hovering nigh
And happy rambles when the roads get dry
The insect world now sunbeams higher climb
Oft dream of spring and wake before their time
Blue flyes from straw stack crawling scarce alive 235
And bees peep out on slabs before the hive
Stroaking their little legs across their wings
And venturing short flight where the snow drop hings
Its silver bell—and winter aconite
Wi buttercup like flowers that shut at night   240
And green leaf frilling round their cups of gold
Like tender maiden muffld from the cold
They sip and find their honey dreams are vain
And feebly hasten to their hives again
And butter flys by eager hopes undone   245
Glad as a child come out to greet the sun
Lost neath the shadow of a sudden shower
Nor left to see tomorrows april flower

APRIL

The infant april joins the spring
And views its watery skye
As youngling linnet trys its wing
And fears at first to flye
With timid step she ventures on   5
And hardly dares to smile
The blossoms open one by one
And sunny hours beguile

But finer days approacheth yet
With scenes more sweet to charm   10
And suns arive that rise and set
Bright strangers to a storm

And as the birds with louder song
Each mornings glory cheers
With bolder step she speeds along   15
And looses all her fears

In wanton gambols like a child
She tends her early toils
And seeks the buds along the wild
That blossom while she smiles   20
And laughing on with nought to chide
She races with the hours
Or sports by natures lovley side
And fills her lap with flowers

Tho at her birth north cutting gales   25
Her beautys oft disguise
And hopfull blossoms turning pale
Upon her bosom dies
Yet ere she seeks another place
And ends her reign in this   30
She leaves us with as fair a face
As ere gave birth to bliss

And fairey month of waking mirth
From whom our joys ensue
Thou early gladder of the earth   35
Thrice welcom here anew
With thee the bud unfolds to leaves
The grass greens on the lea
And flowers their tender boon recieves
To bloom and smile with thee   40

The shepherds on thy pasture walks
The first fair cows lip finds
Whose tufted flowers on slender stalks
Keep nodding to the winds
And tho thy thorns withold the may   45
Their shades the violets bring
Which childern stoop for in their play
As tokens of the spring

The time when daiseys bloom divine
With thy calm hours begun   50
And crowflowers blazing blooms are thine
Bright childern of the sun
Along thy woodlands shaded nooks
The primrose wanly comes
And shining in thy pebley brooks   55
The horse bleb gaily blooms

The long lost charm of sparkling dew
Thy gentle birth recieves
And on thy wreathing locks we view
The first infolding leaves   60
And seeking firstling buds and flowers
The trials of thy skill
Were pastimes of my infant hours
And so they haunt me still

To see thy first broad arum leaves   65
I lovd them from a child
And where thy woodbines sprouting weaves
I joyd to trace the wild

And jocund as thy lambs at play
I met the wanton wind   70
With feelings that have passd away
Whose shadows cling behind

Those joys which childhood claims its own
Woud they were kin to men
Those treasures to the world unknown 75
When known—was witherd then
But hovering round our growing years
To gild cares sable shroud
Their spirit thro the gloom appears
As suns behind a cloud   80

As thou first met my infant eyes
When thro thy fields I flew
Whose distance where they meet the skyes
Was all the worlds I knew
That warmth of fancys wildest hours 85
Which made things kin to life
That heard a voice in trees and flowers
Has swoond in reasons strife

Sweet month thy pleasures bids thee be
The fairest child of spring   90
And every hour that comes with thee
Comes some new joy to bring
The trees still deepen in their bloom
Grass greens the meadow lands
And flowers with every morning come 95
As dropt by fairey hands

APRIL

The field and gardens lovley hours
Begin and end with thee
For whats so sweet as peeping flowers
And bursting buds to see   100
What time the dews unsullied drops
In burnishd gold distills
On crocus flowers unclosing tops
And drooping daffodills

Each day with added glorys come   105
And as they leave the night
Put on the roseys lovley bloom
And blushes with delight
And suns that wait their welcome birth
With earlier haste pursue   110
Their journeys to this lower earth
To free their steps from dew

To see thee come all hearts rejoice
And warms with feelings strong
With thee all nature finds a voice   115
And hums a waking song
The lover views thy welcome hours
And thinks of summer come
And takes the maid thy early flowers
To tempt her steps from home   120

Along each hedge and sprouting bush
The singing birds are blest
And linnet green and speckld thrush
Prepare their mossy nest

On the warm bed thy plain supplys   125
The young lambs find repose
And mid thy green hills basking lies
Like spots of lingering snows

Young things of tender life again
Enjoys thy sunny hours   130
And gosslings waddle oer the plain
As yellow as its flowers
Or swim the pond in wild delight
To catch the water flye
Where hissing geese in ceasless spite   135
Make childern scamper bye

Again the fairey tribes pursue
Their pleasures on the plain
And brightend with the morning dew
Black circles shine again   140
And on its superstitious ground
Where flowers seem loath to dwell
The toadstools fuzzy balls abound
And mushrooms yearly swell

The seasons beautys all are thine   145
That visit with the year
Beautys that poets think divine
And all delight to hear
Thy latter days a pleasure brings
That gladden every heart   150
Pleasures that come like lovley things
But like to shades depart

43

Thy opend leaves and ripend buds
The cuckoo makes his choice
And shepherds in thy greening woods   155
First hears the cheering voice
And to thy ripend blooming bowers
The nightingale belongs
And singing to thy parting hours
Keeps night awake with songs   160

With thee the swallow dares to come
And prunes his sutty wings
And urgd to seek their yearly home
Thy suns the Martin brings
And lovley month be leisure mine   165
Thy yearly mate to be
Tho may day scenes may brighter shine
Their birth belongs to thee

I waked me with thy rising sun
And thy first glorys viewd   170
And as thy welcome hours begun
Their sunny steps pursued
And now thy sun is on the set
Like to a lovley eve
I view thy parting with regret   175
And linger loath to leave

Thou lovley april fare thee well
Thou early child of spring
Tho born where storms too often dwell
Thy parcnts news to bring   180

44

APRIL

Yet what thy parting youth supplys
No other months excell
Thou first for flowers and sunny skyes
Sweet april fare thee well

MAY

Come queen of months in company
Wi all thy merry minstrelsy
The restless cuckoo absent long
And twittering swallows chimney song
And hedge row crickets notes that run   5
From every bank that fronts the sun
And swathy bees about the grass
That stops wi every bloom they pass
And every minute every hour
Keep teazing weeds that wear a flower   10
And toil and childhoods humming joys
For there is music in the noise

The village childern mad for sport
In school times leisurc ever short
That cuck and catch the bouncing ball   15
And run along the church yard wall
Capt wi rude figured slabs whose claims
In times bad memory hath no names
Oft racing round the nookey church
Or calling ecchos in the porch   20
And jelting oer the weather cock
Viewing wi jealous eyes the clock
Oft leaping grave stones leaning hights
Uncheckt wi mellancholy sights
The green grass swelld in many a heap   25
Where kin and friends and parents sleep
Unthinking in their jovial cry
That time shall come when they shall lye
As lonly and as still as they
While other boys above them play   30
Heedless as they do now to know
The unconcous dust that lies below
The shepherd goes wi happy stride
Wi morns long shadow by his side
Down the dryd lanes neath blooming may   35
That once was over shoes in clay
While martins twitter neath his eaves
Which he at early morning leaves
The driving boy beside his team
Will oer the may month beauty dream   40
And cock his hat and turn his eye
On flower and tree and deepning skye

And oft bursts loud in fits of song
And whistles as he reels along
Cracking his whip in starts of joy   45
A happy dirty driving boy
The youth who leaves his corner stool
Betimes for neighbouring village school
While as a mark to urge him right
The church spires all the way in sight   50
Wi cheerings from his parents given
Starts neath the joyous smiles of heaven
And sawns wi many an idle stand
Wi bookbag swinging in his hand
And gazes as he passes bye   55
On every thing that meets his eye
Young lambs seem tempting him to play
Dancing and bleating in his way
Wi trembling tails and pointed ears
They follow him and loose their fears   60
He smiles upon their sunny faces
And feign woud join their happy races
The birds that sing on bush and tree
Seem chirping for his company
And all in fancys idle whim   65
Seem keeping holiday but him
He lolls upon each resting stile
To see the fields so sweetly smile
To see the wheat grow green and long
And list the weeders toiling song   70
Or short note of the changing thrush
Above him in the white thorn bush

That oer the leaning stile bends low
Loaded wi mockery of snow
Mozzld wi many a lushy thread 75
Of crab tree blossoms delicate red
He often bends wi many a wish
Oer the brig rail to view the fish
Go sturting by in sunny gleams
And chucks in the eye dazzld streams 80
Crumbs from his pocket oft to watch
The swarming struttle come to catch
Them where they to the bottom sile
Sighing in fancys joy the while
Hes cautiond not to stand so nigh 85
By rosey milkmaid tripping bye
Where he admires wi fond delight
And longs to be their mate till night
He often ventures thro the day
At truant now and then to play 90
Rambling about the field and plain
Seeking larks nests in the grain
And picking flowers and boughs of may
To hurd awhile and throw away
Lurking neath bushes from the sight 95
Of tell tale eyes till schools noon night[1]
Listning each hour for church clocks hum
To know the hour to wander home
That parents may not think him long
Nor dream of his rude doing wrong 100
Dreading thro night wi dreaming pain
To meet his masters wand again

[1] i.e. when school ends (night) at noon.

Each hedge is loaded thick wi green
And where the hedger late hath been
Tender shoots begin to grow   105
From the mossy stumps below
While sheep and cow that teaze the grain
Will nip them to the root again
They lay their bill and mittens bye
And on to other labours hie   110
While wood men still on spring intrudes
And thins the shadow solitudes
Wi sharpend axes felling down
The oak trees budding into brown
Where as they crash upon the ground   115
A crowd of labourers gather round
And mix among the shadows dark
To rip the crackling staining bark
From off the tree and lay when done
The rolls in lares to meet the sun   120
Depriving yearly where they come
The green wood pecker of its home
That early in the spring began
Far from the sight of troubling man
And bord their round holes in each tree   125
In fancys sweet security
Till startld wi the woodmans noise
It wakes from all its dreaming joys
The blue bells too that thickly bloom
Where man was never feard to come   130
And smell smocks that from view retires
Mong rustling leaves and bowing briars

And stooping lilys of the valley
That comes wi shades and dews to dally
While beady drops on slender threads   135
Wi broad hood leaves above their heads
Like white robd maids in summer hours
Neath umberellas shunning showers
These neath the barkmens crushing treads
Oft perish in their blooming beds   140
Thus stript of boughs and bark in white
Their trunks shine in the mellow light
Beneath the green surviving trees
That wave above them in the breeze
And waking whispers slowly bends   145
As if they mournd their fallen friends
Each morning now the weeders meet
To cut the thistle from the wheat
And ruin in the sunny hours
Full many wild weeds of their flowers   150
Corn poppys that in crimson dwell
Calld 'head achs' from their sickly smell
And carlock yellow as the sun
That oer the may fields thickly run
And 'iron weed' content to share   155
The meanest spot that spring can spare
Een roads where danger hourly comes
Is not wi out its purple blooms
And leaves wi pricks like thistles round
Thick set that have no strength to wound   160
That shrink to childhoods eager hold
Like hair—and with its eye of gold

And scarlet starry points of flowers
Pimpernel dreading nights and showers
Oft calld 'the shepherds weather glass'   165
That sleep till suns have dryd the grass
Then wakes and spreads its creeping bloom
Till clouds or threatning shadows come
Then close it shuts to sleep again
Which weeders see and talk of rain   170
And boys that mark them shut so soon
Will call them 'John go bed at noon'
And fumitory too a name
That superstition holds to fame
Whose red and purple mottld flowers   175
Are cropt by maids in weeding hours
To boil in water milk and whey[1]
For washes on an holiday
To make their beauty fair and sleak
And scour the tan from summers cheek   180
And simple small forget me not
Eyd wi a pinshead yellow spot
Ith[2] middle of its tender blue
That gains from poets notice due
These flowers their toil by crowds destroys 185
And robs them of their lonly joys
That met the may wi hopes as sweet
As those her suns in gardens meet
And oft the dame will feel inclind
As childhoods memory comes to mind   190
To turn her hook away and spare
The blooms it lovd to gather there

[1] Clare has 'way'.   [2] = In the.

My wild field catalogue of flowers
Grows in my ryhmes as thick as showers
Tedious and long as they may be   195
To some they never weary me
Then wood and mead and field of grain
I coud hunt oer and oer again
And talk to every blossom wild
Fond as a parent to a child   200
And cull them in my childish joy
By swarms and swarms and never cloy
When their lank shades oer morning pearls
Shrink from their lengths to little girls
And like the clock hand pointing one   205
Is turned and tells the morning gone
They leave their toils for dinners hour
Beneath some hedges bramble bower
And season sweet their savory meals
Wi joke and tale and merry peals   210
Of ancient tunes from happy tongues
While linnets join their fitful songs
Perchd oer their heads in frolic play
Among the tufts of motling may
The young girls whisper things of love   215
And from the old dames hearing move
Oft making 'love knotts' in the shade
Of blue green oat or wheaten blade
And trying simple charms and spells
That rural superstition tells   220
They pull the little blossom threads
From out the knopweeds button heads

And put the husk wi many a smile
In their white bosoms for awhile
Who if they guess aright the swain   225
That loves sweet fancys trys to gain
Tis said that ere its lain an hour
Twill blossom wi a second flower
And from her white breasts hankerchief
Bloom as they ne'er had lost a leaf   230
When signs appear that token wet
As they are neath the bushes met
The girls are glad wi hopes of play
And harping of the holiday
A hugh blue bird will often swim   235
Along the wheat when skys grow dim
Wi clouds—slow as the gales of spring
In motion wi dark shadowd wing
Beneath the coming storm it sails
And lonly chirps the wheat hid quails   240
That come to live wi spring again
And start when summer browns the grain
They start the young girls joys afloat
Wi 'wet my foot' its yearly note
So fancy doth the sound explain   245
And proves it oft a sign of rain
About the moor mong sheep and cow
The boy or old man wanders now
Hunting all day wi hopful pace
Each thick sown rushy thistly place   250
For plover eggs while oer them flye
The fearful birds wi teazing cry

Trying to lead their steps astray
And coying him another way
And be the weather chill or warm   255
Wi brown hats truckd beneath his arm
Holding each prize their search has won
They plod bare headed to the sun
Now dames oft bustle from their wheels
Wi childern scampering at their heels   260
To watch the bees that hang and snive
In clumps about each thronging hive
And flit and thicken in the light
While the old dame enjoys the sight
And raps the while their warming pans   265
A spell that superstition plans
To coax them in the gardens bounds
As if they lovd the tinkling sounds
And oft one hears the dinning noise
Which dames believe each swarm decoys   270
Around each village day by day
Mingling in the warmth of may
Sweet scented herbs her skill contrives
To rub the bramble platted hives
Fennels thread leaves and crimpld balm   275
To scent the new house of the swarm
The thresher dull as winter days
And lost to all that spring displays
Still mid his barn dust forcd to stand
Swings his frail round wi weary hand   280
While oer his head shades thickly creep
And hides the blinking owl asleep

And bats in cobweb corners bred
Sharing till night their murky bed
The sunshine trickles on the floor   285
Thro every crivice of the door
And makes his barn where shadows dwell
As irksome as a prisoners cell
And as he seeks his daily meal
As schoolboys from their tasks will steal   290
He often stands in fond delay
To see the daisey in his way
And wild weeds flowering on the wall
That will his childish sports recall
Of all the joys that came wi spring   295
The twirling top the marble ring
The gingling halfpence hussld up
At pitch and toss the eager stoop
To pick up heads, the smuggld plays
Neath hovels upon sabbath days   300
When parson he is safe from view
And clerk sings amen in his pew
The sitting down when school was oer
Upon the threshold by his door
Picking from mallows sport to please   305
Each crumpld seed he calld a cheese
And hunting from the stackyard sod
The stinking hen banes velted pod
By youths vain fancys sweetly fed
Christning them his loaves of bread   310
He sees while rocking down the street
Wi weary hands and crimpling feet

Young childern at the self same games
And hears the self same simple names
Still floating on each happy tongue   315
Touchd wi the simple scene so strong
Tears almost start and many a sigh
Regrets the happiness gone bye
And in sweet natures holiday
His heart is sad while all is gay   320
How lovly now are lanes and balks
For toils and lovers sunday walks
The daisey and the buttercup
For which the laughing childern stoop
A hundred times throughout the day   325
In their rude ramping summer play
So thickly now the pasture crowds
In gold and silver sheeted clouds
As if the drops in april showers
Had woo'd the sun and swoond to flowers   330
The brook resumes its summer dresses
Purling neath grass and water cresses
And mint and flag leaf swording high
Their blooms to the unheeding eye
And taper bowbent hanging rushes   335
And horse tail childerns bottle brushes
And summer tracks about its brink
Is fresh agen where cattle drink
And on its sunny bank the swain
Stretches his idle length again   340
Soon as the sun forgets the day
The moon looks down on the lovly may

And the little star his friend and guide
Travelling together side by side
And the seven stars and charleses wain[1]   345
Hangs smiling oer green woods again
The heaven rekindles all alive
Wi light the may bees round the hive
Swarm not so thick in mornings eye
As stars do in the evening skye   350
All all are nestling in their joys
The flowers and birds and pasture boys
The fire tail long a stranger comes
To his last summer haunts and homes
To hollow tree and crevisd wall   355
And in the grass the rails odd call
That featherd spirit stops the swain
To listen to his note again
And school boy still in vain retraces
The secrets of his hiding places   360
In the black thorns crowded copse
Thro its varied turns and stops
The nightingale its ditty weaves
Hid in a multitude of leaves
The boy stops short to hear the strain   365
And 'sweet jug jug' he mocks again
The yellow hammer builds its nest
By banks where sun beams earliest rest
That drys the dews from off the grass
Shading it from all that pass   370
Save the rude boy wi ferret gaze
That hunts thro evry secret maze

[1] Charles's Wain = The Plough.

He finds its pencild eggs agen
All streakd wi lines as if a pen
By natures freakish hand was took   375
To scrawl them over like a book
And from these many mozzling marks
The school boy names them 'writing larks'
Bum barrels twit on bush and tree
Scarse bigger then a bumble bee   380
And in a white thorns leafy rest
It builds its curious pudding-nest
Wi hole beside as if a mouse
Had built the little barrel house
Toiling full many a lining feather   385
And bits of grey tree moss together
Amid the noisey rooky park
Beneath the firdales branches dark
The little golden crested wren
Hangs up his gluing nest agen   390
And sticks it to the furry leaves
As martins theirs beneath the eaves
The old hens leave the roost betimes
And oer the garden pailing climbs
To scrat the gardens fresh turnd soil   395
And if unwatchd his crops to spoil
Oft cackling from the prison yard
To peck about the homclose sward
Catching at butterflys and things
Ere they have time to try their wings   400
The cattle feels the breath of may
And kick and toss their heads in play

The ass beneath his bags of sand
Oft jerks the string from leaders hand
And on the road will eager stoop   405
To pick the sprouting thistle up
Oft answering on his weary way
Some distant neighbours sobbing bray
Dinning the ears of driving boy
As if he felt a fit of joy   410
Wi in its pinfold circle left
Of all its company bereft
Starvd stock no longer noising round
Lone in the nooks of foddering ground
Each skeleton of lingering stack   415
By winters tempests beaten black
Nodds upon props or bolt upright
Stands swarthy in the summer light
And oer the green grass seems to lower
Like stump of old time wasted tower   420
All that in winter lookd for hay
Spread from their batterd haunts away
To pick the grass or lye at lare
Beneath the mild hedge shadows there
Sweet month that gives a welcome call   425
To toil and nature and to all
Yet one day mid thy many joys
Is dead to all its sport and noise
Old may day wheres thy glorys gone
All fled and left thee every one   430
Thou comst to thy old haunts and homes
Unnoticd as a stranger comes

No flowers arc pluckt to hail thee now
Nor cotter seeks a single bough
The maids no more on thy sweet morn   435
Awake their thresholds to adorn
Wi dewey flowers—May locks new come
And princifeathers cluttering bloom
And blue bells from the wood land moss
And cowslip cucking balls to toss   440
Above the garlands swinging hight
Hang in the soft eves sober light
These maid and child did yearly pull
By many a folded apron full
But all is past the merry song   445
Of maidens hurrying along
To crown at eve the earliest cow
Is gone and dead and silent now
The laugh raisd at the mawking thorn
Tyd to the cows tail last that morn   450
The kerchief at arms length displayd
Held up by pairs of swain and maid
While others bolted underneath
Bawling loud wi panting breath
'Duck under water' as they ran   455
Alls ended as[1] they ne'er began
While the new thing that took thy place
Wears faded smiles upon its face
And where enclosure has its birth
It spreads a mildew oer her mirth   460
The herd no longer one by one
Goes plodding on her morning way

[1] = as if.

61

And garlands lost and sports nigh gone
Leaves her like thee a common day
Yet summer smiles upon thee still   465
Wi natures sweet unalterd will
And at thy births unworshipd hours
Fills her green lap wi swarms of flowers
To crown thee still as thou hast been
Of spring and summers months the queen   470

JUNE

Now summer is in flower and natures hum
Is never silent round her sultry bloom
Insects as small as dust are never done
Wi glittering dance and reeling in the sun
And green wood fly and blossom haunting bee   5
Are never weary of their melody
Round field hedge now flowers in full glory twine
Large bindweed bells wild hop and streakd woodbine
That lift athirst their slender throated flowers
Agape for dew falls and for honey showers   10

These round each bush in sweet disorder run
And spread their wild hues to the sultry sun
Where its silk netting lace on twigs and leaves
The mottld spider at eves leisure weaves
That every morning meet the poets eye   15
Like faireys dew wet dresses hung to dry
The wheat swells into ear and leaves below
The may month wild flowers and their gaudy show
Bright carlock bluecap and corn poppy red
Which in such clouds of colors widely spread   20
That at the sun rise might to fancys eye
Seem to reflect the many colord sky
And leverets seat and lark and partridge nest
It leaves a schoolboys height in snugger rest
And oer the weeders labour overgrows   25
Who now in merry groups each morning goes
To willow skirted meads wi fork and rake
The scented hay cocks in long rows to make
Where their old visitors in russet brown
The hay time butterflyes dance up and down   30
And gads that teaze like whasps the timid maid
And drive the herdboys cows to pond and shade
Who when his dogs assistance fails to stop
Is forcd his half made oaten pipes to drop
And start and halloo thro the dancing heat   35
To keep their gadding tumult from the wheat
Who in their rage will dangers overlook
And leap like hunters oer the pasture brook
Brushing thro blossomd beans in maddening haste
And stroying corn they scarce can stop to taste   40

Labour pursues its toil in weary mood
And feign woud rest wi shadows in the wood
The mowing gangs bend oer the beeded grass
Where oft the gipseys hungry journeying ass
Will turn its wishes from the meadow paths   45
Listning the rustle of the falling swaths
The ploughman sweats along the fallow vales
And down the suncrackt furrow slowly trails
Oft seeking when athirst the brooks supply
Where brushing eager the brinks bushes bye   50
For coolest water he oft brakes[1] the rest
Of ring dove brooding oer its idle nest
And there as loath to leave the swaily place
He'll stand to breath and whipe his burning face
The shepherds idle hours are over now   55
Nor longer leaves him neath the hedgrow bough
On shadow pillowd banks and lolling stile
Wilds looses now their summer friends awhile
Shrill whistles barking dogs and chiding scold
Drive bleating sheep each morn from fallow fold   60
To wash pits where the willow shadows lean
Dashing them in their fold staind coats to clean
Then turnd on sunny sward to dry agen
They drove them homward to the clipping pen
In hurdles pent where elm or sycamore   65
Shut out the sun—or in some threshing floor
There they wi scraps of songs and laugh and tale
Lighten their anual toils while merry ale
Goes round and gladdens old mens hearts to praise
The thread bare customs of old farmers days   70

[1] = breaks.

Who while the sturting sheep wi trembling fears
Lies neath the snipping of his harmless sheers
Recalls full many a thing by bards unsung
And pride forgot—that reignd when he was young
How the hugh bowl was in the middle set   75
At breakfast time as clippers yearly met
Filld full of frumity where yearly swum
The streaking sugar and the spotting plumb
Which maids coud never to the table bring
Without one rising from the merry ring   80
To lend a hand who if twas taen amiss
Woud sell his kindness for a stolen kiss
The large stone pitcher in its homly trim
And clouded pint horn wi its copper rim
Oer which rude healths was drank in spirits high   85
From the best broach the cellar woud supply
While sung the ancient swains in homly ryhmes
Songs that were pictures of the good old times
When leathern bottles held the beer nut brown
That wakd the sun wi songs and sung him down   90
Thus will the old man ancient ways bewail
Till toiling sheers gain ground upon the tale
And brakes it off—when from the timid sheep
The fleece is shorn and wi a fearfull leap
He starts—while wi a pressing hand   95
His sides are printed by the tarry brand
Shaking his naked skin wi wondering joys
And fresh ones are tugd in by sturdy boys
Who when theyre thrown down neath the sheering
     swain

Will wipe his brow and start his tale again   100
Tho fashions haughty frown hath thrown aside
Half the old forms simplicity supplyd
Yet there are some prides winter deigns to spare
Left like green ivy when the trees are bare
And now when sheering of the flocks are done   105
Some ancient customs mixd wi harmless fun
Crowns the swains merry toils—the timid maid
Pleasd to be praisd and yet of praise affraid
Seeks her best flowers not those of woods and fields
But such as every farmers garden yields   110
Fine cabbage roses painted like her face
And shining pansys trimd in golden lace
And tall tuft larkheels featherd thick wi flowers
And woodbines climbing oer the door in bowers
And London tufts of many a mottld hue   115
And pale pink pea and monkshood darkly blue
And white and purple jiliflowers that stay
Lingering in blossom summer half away
And single blood walls of a lucious smell
Old fashiond flowers which hus wives love so well   120
And columbines stone blue or deep night brown
Their honey-comb-like blossoms hanging down
Each cottage gardens fond adopted child
Tho heaths still claim them where they yet grow wild
Mong their old wild companions summer blooms   125
Furze brake and mozzling ling and golden broom
Snap dragons gaping like to sleepy clowns
And 'clipping pinks' (which maidens sunday gowns
Full often wear catcht at by toying chaps)

Pink as the ribbons round their snowy caps 130
'Bess in her bravery' too of glowing dyes
As deep as sunsets crimson pillowd skyes
And majoram notts sweet briar and ribbon grass
And lavender the choice of every lass
And sprigs of lads love all familiar names 135
Which every garden thro the village claims
These the maid gathers wi a coy delight
And tyes them up in readiness for night
Giving to every swain tween love and shame
Her 'clipping poseys' as their yearly claim 140
And turning as he claims the custom kiss
Wi stifld smiles half ankering after bliss
She shrinks away and blushing calls it rude
But turns to smile and hopes to be pursued
While one to whom the seeming hint applied 145
Follows to claim it and is not denyd
No doubt a lover for within his coat
His nosgay owns each flower of better sort
Ancl when the envious mutter oer their beer
And nodd the secret to his neighbor near 150
Raising the laugh to make the matter known
She blushes silent and will not disown
And ale and songs and healths and merry ways
Keeps up a shadow of old farmers days
But the old beachen bowl that once supplyd 155
Its feast of frumity is thrown aside
And the old freedom that was living then
When masters made them merry wi their men
Whose coat was like his neighbors russet brown

And whose rude speech was vulgar as his clown   160
Who in the same hour drank the rest among
And joind the chorus while a labourer sung
All this is past—and soon may pass away
The time torn remnant of the holiday
As proud distinction makes a wider space   165
Between the genteel and the vulgar race
Then must they fade as pride oer custom showers
Its blighting mildew on her feeble flowers

JULY

Daughter of pastoral smells and sights
And sultry days and dewy nights
July resumes her yearly place
Wi her milking maiden face
Ruddy and tannd yet sweet to view   5
When everywheres a veil of dew
And raps[1] it round her looks that smiles
A lovly rest to daily toils
Wi last months closing scenes and dins
Her sultry beaming birth begins   10

Hay makers still in grounds appear
And some are thinning nearly clear

[1] = wraps.

70

Save oddly lingering shocks about
Which the tithman counteth out
Sticking their green boughs where they go   15
The parsons yearly claims to know
Which farmers view wi grudging eye
And grumbling drive their waggons bye
In hedge bound close and meadow plains
Stript groups of busy bustling swains   20
From all her hants wi noises rude
Drives to the wood lands solitude
That seeks a spot unmarkd wi paths
Far from the close and meadow swaths
Wi smutty song and story gay   25
They cart the witherd smelling hay
Boys loading on the waggon stand
And men below wi sturdy hand
Heave up the shocks on lathy prong
While horse boys lead the team along   30
And maidens drag the rake behind
Wi light dress shaping to the wind
And trembling locks of curly hair
And snow white bosoms nearly bare
That charms ones sight amid the hay   35
Like lingering blossoms of the may
From clowns rude jokes they often turn
And oft their cheeks wi blushes burn
From talk which to escape a sneer
They oft affect as not to hear   40
Some in the nooks about the ground
Pile up the stacks swelld bellying round

The milking cattles winter fare
That in the snow are fodderd there
Warm spots wi black thorn thickets lind   45
And trees to brake[1] the northern wind
While masters oft the sultry hours
Will urge their speed and talk of showers
When boy from home trotts to the stack
Wi dinner upon dobbins back   50
And bottles to the saddle tyd
Or ballancd upon either side
A horse thats past his toiling day
Yet still a favorite in his way
That trotts on errands up and down   55
The fields and too and fro from town
Long ere his presence comes in sight
Boys listen wi heart felt delight
And know his footsteps down the road
Hastening wi the dinner load   60
Then they seek in close or meadows
High hedgerows wi grey willow shadows
To hide beneath from sultry noon
And rest them at their dinner boon
Where helping shepherd for the lass   65
Will seek a hillock on the grass
The thickset hedge or stack beside
Where teazing pismires ne'er abide
And when tis found down drops the maid
Proud wi the kind attention paid   70
And still the swain wi notice due
Waits on her all the dinner through

[1] = break.

And fills her horn which she tho dry
In shoyness often pushes bye
While he will urge wi many a smile   75
It as a strength to help her toil
And in her hand will oft contrive
From out his pocket pulld to slive
Stole fruit when no one turns his eye
To wet her mouth when shes adry   80
Offerd when she refuses ale
Noons sultry labour to regale
Teazd wi the countless multitude
Of flyes that every where intrude
While boys wi boughs will often try   85
To beat them from them as they lye
Who find their labour all in vain
And soon as scard they swarm again
Thus while each swain and boy and lass
Sit at their dinner on the grass   90
The teams wi gears thrown on their backs
Stand pulling at the shocks or racks
Switching their tails and turning round
To knap the gadflys teazing wound
While dob that brought the dinners load   95
Too tricky to be turnd abroad
Needing the scuttle shook wi grain
To coax him to be caught again
Is to a tree at tether tyd
Ready for boy to mount and ride   100
Nipping the grass about his pound
And stamping battering hooves around

Soon as each ground is clear of hay
The shepherd whoops his flocks away
From fallow fields to plentys scenes   105
Shining as smooth as bowling greens
But scard wi clipping tides alarms
They bleat about the close in swarms
And hide neath hedges in the cool
Still panting tho wi out their whool   110
Markd wi the tard brands lasting dye
And make a restless hue and cry
Answering the lambs that call again
And for their old dams seek in vain
Running mid the stranger throng   115
And ever meeting wi the wrong
Fiegn[1] wi some old yoe to abide
Who smells and tosses them aside
And some as if they knew its face
Will meet a lamb wi mended pace   120
But proving hopes indulgd in vain
They turn around and blair again
Till weand from memory half forgot
They spread and feed and notice not
Save now and then to lambs shrill crys   125
Odd yoes in hoarser tone replys
Still may be seen the mowing swain
On balks between the fields of grain
Who often stops his thirst to ease
To pick the juicy pods of pease   130
And oft as chances bring to pass
Stoops oer his scythe stick in the grass

[1] = Feign = Fain.

To suck the brimming honey comb
Which bees so long were toiling home
And rifld from so many flowers   135
And carried thro so many hours
He tears their small hives mossy ball
Where the brown labourers hurded all
Who gather homward one by one
And see their nest and honey gone   140
Humming around his rushy toil
Their mellancholly wrongs awhile
Then oer the sweltering swaths they stray
And hum disconsolate away
And oft neath hedges cooler screen   145
Where meadow sorrel lingers green
Calld 'sour grass' by the knowing clown
The mower gladly chews it down
And slakes his thirst the best he may
When singing brooks are far away   150
And his hoopd bottle woeful tale
Is emptied of its cheering ale
That lulld him in unconscous sleep
At dinners hour beneath a heap
Of grass or bush or edding shock   155
Till startld by the country clock
That told the hour his toil had lost
Who coud but spare an hour at most
And wearing past the setting sun
He stays to get his labour done   160
The gipsey down the meadow brook
Wi long pole and a reaping hook

Tyd at its end amid the streams
That glitters wi the hot sunbeams
Reaches and cuts the bulrush down   165
And hawks them round each neighboring town
Packd at his back or tyd in loads
On asses down the dusty roads
He jogs and shouts from door to door
His well known note of calling oer   170
Offering to hus wives cheap repairs
Mending their broken bottomd chairs
Wi step half walk half dance and eye
Ready to smile on passers bye
Wi load well suiting weather warm   175
Tuckd carlessly beneath his arm
Or peeping coat and side between
In woolen bag of faded green
Half conseald and half displayd
A purpose tell tale to his trade   180
The gipsey fiddler jogs away
To village feast and holiday
Scraping in public house to trye
What beer his music will supply
From clowns who happy wi the din   185
Dance their hard naild hilos thin
Along the roads in passing crowds
Followd by dust like smoaking clouds
Scotch droves of beast a little breed
In swelterd weary mood proceed   190
A patient race from scottish hills
To fatten by our pasture rills

Lean wi the wants of mountain soil
But short and stout for travels toil
Wi cockd up horns and curly crown 195
And dewlap bosom hanging down
Followd by slowly pacing swains
Wild to our rushy flats and plains
At whom the shepherds dog will rise
And shake himself and in supprise 200
Draws back and waffles in affright
Barking the traveller out of sight
And mowers oer their scythes will bear
Upon their uncooth dress to stare
And shepherds as they trample bye 205
Leaves oer their hooks a wondering eye
To witness men so oddly clad
In petticoats of banded plad
Wi blankets oer their shoulders slung
To camp at night the fields among 210
When they for rest on commons stop
And blue cap like a stocking top
Cockt oer their faces summer brown
Wi scarlet tazzeles on the crown
Rude patterns of the thistle flower 215
Unbrinkd and open to the shower
And honest faces frank and free
That breathe of mountain liberty
Soon as the morning wakens red
The shepherd startles from his bed 220
And rocks afield his morning pace
While[1] folded sheep will know his face

[1] See Glossary.

77

Rising as he appears in sight
To shake their coats as in delight
His shadow stalking stride for stride   225
Stretches a jiant by his side
Long as a tree without a top
And oft it urges him to stop
Both in his journey and his song
And wonders why it seems so long   230
And bye and bye as mornïng dies
Shrinks to an unbrichd boy in size
Then as the evening gathers blue
Grows to a jiants length anew
Puzzld the more he stops to pause   235
His wisdom vainly seeks the cause
Again his journey he pursues
Lengthening his track along the dews
And his dog that turnd to pick
From his sides the sucking tick   240
Insects that on cattle creep
And bites the labourer laid asleep
Pricks up his ears to see him gone
And shakes his hide and hastens on
And the while the shepherd stayd   245
Trailing a track the hare had made
Bolts thro the creeping hedge again
And hurrying follows wi the swain
The singing shouting herding boys
Follows again their wild employs   250
And ere the sun puts half his head
From out his crimson pillowd bed

And bawls behind his cows again
That one by one lobs down the lane
Wi wild weeds in his hat anew   255
The summer sorts of every hue
And twigs of leaves that please his eye
To his old haunts he hallows bye
Wi dog that loiters by his side
Or trotts before wi nimble stride   260
That waits till bid to bark and run
And panteth from the dreaded sun
And oft amid the sunny day
Will join a partner in his play
And in his antic tricks and glee   265
Will prove as fond of sport as he
And by the flag pool summer warm
He'll watch the motions of his arm
That holds a stick or stone to throw
In the sun gilded flood below   270
And head oer ears he danses in
Nor fears to wet his curly skin
The boys peeld cudgel to restore
And brings it in his mouth ashore
And eager as for crust or bone   275
He'll run to catch the pelted stone
Till wearied out he shakes his hide
And drops his tail and sneaks aside
Unheeding whistles shouts and calls
To take a rest where thickly falls   280
The rush clumps shadows there he lyes
Licking his skin and catching flyes

Or picking tween his stretching feet
The bone he had not time to eat
Before when wi the teazing boy   285
He was so throngd wi plays employ
Noon gathers wi its blistering breath
Around and day dyes still as death
The breeze is stopt the lazy bough
Hath not a leaf that dances now   290
The totter grass upon the hill
And spiders threads is hanging still
The feathers dropt from morehens wings
Upon the waters surface clings
As stedfast and as heavy seem   295
As stones beneath them in the stream
Hawkweed and groundsels fairey downs
Unruffld keep their seeding crowns
And in the oven heated air
Not one light thing is floating there   300
Save that to the earnest eye
The restless heat swims twittering bye
The swine run restless down the street
Anxious some pond or ditch to meet
From days hot swoonings to retire   305
Wallowing in the weeds and mire
The linnets seek the twiggs that lye
Close to the brook and brig stones drye
At top and sit and dip their bills
Till they have drunk their little fills   310
Then flert their wings and wet their feathers
To cool them in the blazing weathers

Dashing the water oer their heads
Then high[1] them to some cooling sheds
Some dark wood glooms about the plain   315
To pick their feathers smooth again
The young quicks branches seem as dead
And scorch from yellow into rcd
Ere autum hath its pencil taen
Their shades in different hues to stain   320
Following behind the cranking ploughs
Whiping oft their sweating brows
The boys lead horses yokd in pairs
To jumping harrows linkd that tears
And teazes the hard clods to dust   325
Placing for showers in hopes their trust
The farmer follows sprinkling round
Wi turnip seed the panting ground
Providing food for beast and sheep
When winters snows are falling deep   330
Oft proving hopes and wishes vain
While clouds disperse that promisd rain
While soon as ere the turnip creeps
From out the crust burnt soil and peeps
Upon the farmers watching eye   335
Tis eaten by the jumping flye
And eager neath the midday sun
Soon as each plough teams toil is done
Scarse waiting till the gears are taen
From off their backs by boy and swain   340
From hay filld racks they turn away
Nor in the stable care to stay

[1] = hie.

Hurrying to the trough to drink
Or from the yard ponds muddy brink
Rush in and wi long winded soak   345
Drink till theyre almost fit to choak
And from the horsbees teazing din
Thrust deep their burning noses in
Almost above their greedy eyes
To cool their mouths and shun the flyes   350
Deaf to the noise the geese will make
That grudge the worthy share they take
Boys now neath green lanes meeting bough
Each noons half holiday from plough
Take out their hungry teams till night   355
That nipp the grass wi eager bite
Wi long tails switching never still
They lunge neath trees when eat their fill
And stamp and switch till closing day
Brushing the teazing flyes away   360
Endless labour all in vain
That start in crowds to turn again
When the sun is sinking down
And dyes more deep the shadows brown
And gradual into slumber glooms   365
How sweet the village evening comes
To weary hinds from toil releasd
And panting sheep and torturd beast
The shepherd long wi heat opprest
Betakes him to his cottage rest   370
And his tird dog that plods along
Wi panting breath and lolling tongue

Runs eager as the brook appears
And dashes in head over ears
Startling reed sparrow broods to flye   375
That in the reed woods slumberd nigh
And water voles in haste to hide
Nibbling the sedges close beside
Lapping while he floats about
To quench his thirst then drabbles out   380
And shakes his coat and like the swain
Is happy night is come again

The beast that to the pond did creep
And rushd in water belly deep
The gad flyes threatning hums to shun   385
And horse bee darting in the sun
Lashing their tails the while they stood
And sprinkling thick their sides wi mud
Snuff the cool air now day is gone
And linger slow and idly on   390
To the pebbly fore to drink
And drop and rest upon its brink
Ruminating on their beds
Calm as the sky above their heads
The horse whose mouth is seldom still   395
Is up and cropping at his will
The moisting grass unteazd and free
In summer eves serenity
Uncheckt by flyes he grazes on
Right happy that the day is gone   400
Ne'er leaving off to turn around

His stooping head to knap the wound
And tail that switchd his sides all day
Is quiet now the suns away
The cowboys as their herd plod on   405
Before them homward one by one
Grows happy as their toil grows short
And full of fancys restless sport
Oft struts along wi sinking day
Acting proud their soldier play   410
Wi peeld bark sash around each waist
And rush caps on each beaver placd
Stuck wi a head aches red cockade
And wooden swords and sticks displayd
For flags—thus march the evening troop   415
While some one strikes a whistle up
And others wi their dinner tins
The evenings falling quiet dins
Patting wi hollow sounding tums
Rude imitating fifes and drums   420
Calling their cows that plod before
Their army marching from the moor
And thus they act till met the town
Carless of laughs from passing clown
Where their dogs too tird for play   425
Loiter on their evening way
Oft rolling on the damping grass
Or stopping wi the milking lass
Waiting a chance the ways conseal
A mouth full from her pails to steal   430
Or dropping down to pick a bone

By hedger from his wallets thrown
Or found upon some greensward platt
Where hay folks at their dinner sat
Sweet comes the cows breath down the lane   435
Steaming the fragrance of the plain
As home they rock and bawling wait
Till boys run to unloose the gate
And from their milksheds all adry
Turn to the pump wi anxious eye   440
Where shoud the maids wi boys repair
To fill the dashing bucket there
They hurry spite of threatning clown
And kick the milkers bucket down
And horses oft wi eager stoop   445
Will bend adown to steal a sup
Watching a moments chance to win
And dip their eager noses in
As by they pass or set it down
To rest or chatter to a clown   450
And knats wi their small slender noise
Bother too the troubld boys
And teaze the cows that while she chides
Will kick and turn to lick their sides
And like so many hanting sprites   455
Will bite and weal the maid anights
Who dreams of love and sleeps so sound
As ne'er to feel each little wound
Till waken by the morning sun
She wonders at the injury done   460
Thinking in fears simplicity

That faireys dreaded mistery
On her white bosom in the dark
Had been and left each blisterd mark
The fox begins his stunt odd bark   465
Down in its dew bed drops the lark
And on the heath amid the gorse
The night hawk sturts the feeding horse
That pricks his ear wi startling eye
And snorts to hear its trembling crye   470
The owlet leaves his ivy tree
And to its hive slow sails the bee
The mower seeks his cloaths and hides
His scythe home bent wi weary strides
And oer his shoulder swings his bag   475
Carrying in hand his empty cag
Hay makers on their homward way
To the fields will often stray
And mong the grain when no one sees
Nestle and fill their laps wi peas   480
Sheep scard wi tweenlight doubting eye
Leap the path and canter bye
Nipping wi moment stoops the plain
And turning quick to gaze again
Till silence upon eve awaits   485
And milkmaids cease to clap the gates
And homward to the town are gone
Wi whispering sweethearts chatting on
And shepherds homward tracks are past
And dogs rude barks are still at last   490
Then down they drop as suits their wills

Or nips the thyme on pismire hills
Where nought is seen but timid hares
That nights sweet welcome gladly shares
And shadows stooping as they stoop   495
Beside them when the moon gets up
Reviving wi the ruddy moon
Thc nightingale resumes his tune
What time the horsboy drives away
His loose teams from the toils of day   500
To crop the closes dewy blade
Where the haystacks fencd and made
Or on the commons bushy plain
To rest till the sun comes again
Whistling and bawling loud and long   505
The burthen of some drawling song
That grows more loud as eve grows late
Yet when he opes the clapping gate
He cant help turning in his joys
To look if his fear wakeing noise   510
Has raisd a mischief in the wind
And wakd a ghost to stalk behind
And when hes turnd them safe aground
And hookd the chain the gate around
Wi quicker speed he homward sings   515
And leaves them in the mushroom rings
Wi the dewdrunk dancing elves
To eat or rest as suits them selves
And as he hastes from labour done
An owlets whoop een makes him run   520
And bats shill flickerings bobbing near

Turns his heart blood cold wi fear
And when at home wi partner ralph
He hugs himself to think hes safe
And tells his tale while others smile   525
Of all he thought and feard the while
The black house bee hath ceasd to sing
And white nosd one wi out a sting
That boys will catch devoid of dread
Are in their little holes abed   530
And martins neath the mossey eaves
Oft startld at the sparrow thieves
That in their house will often peep
Breaking their little weary sleep
And oft succeed when left alone   535
In making their clay huts their own
Where the cock sparrow on the scout
Watches and keeps the owner out
The geese have left the home close moats
And at the yard gate clean their coats   540
Or neath their feathers tuck their heads
Asleep till driven to their sheds
The pigeon droves in whisking flight
Hurrying to their cotes ere night
In coveys round the village meet   545
And in the dove cote holes retreat
Nor more about the wheaten grounds
The bird boys bell and clapper sounds
Retiring wi the setting sun
His toil and shout and song is done   550
The shill bat wi its flittering mate

Starts thro the church vaults iron grate
Deaths daily visitors and all
He meets save slanting suns that fall
At eve as if they lovd to shed   555
Their daily memory oer the dead
Hodge neath the climbing elms that drop
Their branches oer a dove cote top
Hath milkd his cows and taken in
On yokes the reeking pales or tin   560
And been across the straw to chain
The hen roost wicket safe again
And done his yard rounds hunting eggs
And taen his hat from off the peggs
To scamper to the circling cross   565
To have a game at pitch and toss
And day boy hath his supper got
Of milk before twas hardly hot
Eager from toil to get away
And join the boys at taw to play   570
Neath black smiths cinder litterd shed
Till the hour to go to bed
Old gossips on their greensward bench
Sit where the hom bound milking wench
Will set her buckets down to rest   575
And be awhile their evening guest
To whom their box is held while she
Takes the smallest nips that be
That soon as snift begins to teaze
And makes her turn away to sneeze   580
While old dames say the sign is plain

That she will dream about her swain
And toss the cloaths from off her bed
And cautions her of roguish ned
Holding their hands agen their hips   585
To laugh as up she starts and trips
In quickend speed along the town
Bidding good night to passing clown

From the black smiths shop the swain
Jogs wi ploughshares laid again   590
And drops them by the stable shed
Where gears on pegs hang over head
Ready for driving boys to take
On fore horse when their toils awake
The kitchen wench wi face red hot   595
As blazing fire neath supper pot
Hath cleand her pails and pansions all
And set them leaning by the wall
And twirld her whool mop clean again
And hung it on the pales to drain   600

Now by the maids requesting smile
The shepherd mounts the wood stack pile
Reard high against the orchard pales
And cause of thorns she oft bewails
Prickd hands and holes in sunday gown   605
He throws the smoothest faggot down
And hawls it in at her desire
Ready for the kitching fire

Beneath the elderns village shade
Oer her well curb leans the maid 610
To draw the brimming bucket up
While passing boy to beg a sup
Will stop his roll or rocking cart
And the maidens gentle heart
Gives ready leave—the eager clown 615
Throws off his hat and stoops adown
Soaking his fill then hastens on
To catch his team already gone
Eager from toil to get release
And in the hay field feed at peace 620

The weary thresher leaves his barn
And emptys from his shoes the corn
That gatherd in them thro the day
And homward bends his weary way
The gardener he is sprinkling showers 625
From watering pans on drooping flowers
And set away his hoe and spade
While goody neath the cottage shade
Sits wi a baskett tween her knees
Ready for supper shelling peas 630
And cobler chatting in the town
Hath put his window shutter down
And the knowing parish clerk
Feign to do his jobs ere dark
Hath timd the church clock to the sun 635
And wound it up for night and done
And turnd the hugh kee in the door

Chatting his evening story oer
Up the street the servant maid
Runs wi her errands long delayd 640
And ere the door she enters in
She stops to right a loosend pin
And smooth wi hasty fingers down
The crumpling creases in her gown
Which Rogers oggles rudly made 645
For may games forfeit never paid
And seizd a kiss against her will
While playing quoits upon the hill
Wi other shepherds laughing nigh
That made her shoy and hurry bye 650
The blacksmiths grizly toil is oer
And shut his hot shops branded door
Folding up his arms to start
And take at ease his evening quart
And farmer giles his business done 655
Wi face a very setting sun
Jogging home on dobbins back
From helping at the clover stack
The horse knows well nor trys to pass
The door where for his custom glass 670
He nightly from the saddle jumps
To slake his thirst or cheer the dumps
Leaving old dob his breath to catch
Wi bridle hanging at the latch
The shepherd too will often spare 675
A sixpence to be merry there
While the dog that trackd his feet

Adown the dusty printed street
Lies as one weary loath to roam
Agen the door to wait him home   680
While the taylors long day thirst
Is still unquenchd tho fit to burst
Whose[1] been at truants merry play
From sheers and bodkin all the day
Still soaks the tankard reeling ripe   685
And scarce can stoop to light his pipe
The labourer sitting by his door
Happy that the day is oer
Is stooping downwards to unloose
His leathern baffles or his shoes   690
Making ready for his rest
Quickly to be the pillows guest
While on mothers lap wi in
The childern each their prayers begin
That taen from play are loath to go   695
And looking round repeating slow
Each prayer they stammer in delay
To gain from bed a longer stay
Goody hath set her spinning bye
Deafend by her chattering pye   700
That calls her up wi hungry rage
To put his supper in the cage
That done she sought a neighbours door
A minutes time to gossip oer
And neath her apron now tis night   705
Huddles for home, her candle light
Hid from the wind—to burn an hour

[1] = who's.

93

JULY

As clouds wi threatend thunder lower
The mastiff from his kennel free
Is now unchaind at liberty   710
In readiness to put to rout
The thieves that night may bring about
Thus evening deepning to a close
Leaves toil and nature to repose

AUGUST

Harvest approaches with its bustling day
The wheat tans brown and barley bleaches grey
In yellow garb the oat land intervenes
And tawney glooms the valley thronged with beans
Silent the village grows, wood wandering dreams   5
Seem not so lonely as its quiet seems
Doors are shut up as on a winters day
And not a child about them lies at play
The dust that winnows neath the breezes feet
Is all that stirs about the silent street   10
Fancy might think that desert spreading fear
Had whisperd terrors into quiets ear

Or plundering armys past the place had come
And drove the lost inhabitants from home
The fields now claim them where a motley crew   15
Of old and young their daily tasks pursue
The barleys beard is grey and wheat is brown
And wakens toil betimes to leave the town
The reapers leave their beds before the sun
And gleaners follow in the toils begun   20
To pick the littered ear the reaper leaves
And glean in open fields among the sheaves
The ruddy child nursed in the lap of care
In toils rude strife to do his little share
Beside his mother poddles oer the land   25
Sun burnt and stooping with a weary hand
Picking his tiney glean of corn or wheat
While crackling stubbles wound his little feet
Full glad he often is to sit awhile
Upon a smooth green baulk to ease his toil   30
And feign would spend an idle hour to play
With insects strangers to the moiling day
Creeping about each rush and grassy stem
And often wishes he was one of them
In weariness of heart that he might lye   35
Hid in the grass from the days burning eye
That raises tender blisters on his skin
Thro holes or openings that have lost a pin
Free from the crackling stubs to toil and glean
And smiles to think how happy he had been   40
Whilst his expecting mother stops to tye
Her handful up and waiting his supply

Misses the idle younker from her side
And shouts of rods and morts of threats beside
Pointing to the grey willows while she tells   45
His fears shall fetch one if he still rebells
Picturing harsh truths in his unpracticed eye
How they who idle in the harvest lye
Shall well deserving in the winter pine
Or hunt the hedges with the birds and swine   50
In vain he wishes that the rushes height
Were tall as trees to hide him from her sight
Leaving his pleasant seat he sighs and rubs
His legs and shows scratchd wounds from piercing
    stubs
To make excuse for play but she disdains   55
His little wounds and smiles while he complains
And as he stoops adown in troubles sore
She sees his grief and bids him sob no more
As bye and bye on the next sabbath day
She'll give him well earned pence as well as play   60
When he may buy almost with out a stint
Sweet candied horehound cakes and pepper mint
Or streaking sticks of lucious lolipop
What ere he chuses from the tempting shop
Wi in whose diamond window shining lyes   65
Things of all sorts to tempt his eager eyes
Rich sugar plumbs in phials shining bright
In every hue young fancys to delight
Coaches and ladys of gilt ginger bread
And downy plumbs and apples streaked with red   70
Such promises all sorrows soon displace

And smiles are instant kindled in his face
Scorning all troubles which he felt before
He picks the trailing ears and mourns no more
The fields are all alive with sultry noise   75
Of labours sounds and insects busy joys
Some oer their glittering sickles stoop
Startling full oft the partridge coveys up
Some oer the rustling scythe go bending on
And shockers follow where their toils have gone   80
First turning swaths to wither in the sun
Where mice from terrors dangers nimbly run
Leaving their tender young in fears alarm
Lapt up in nests of chimbled grasses warm
And oft themselves for safty search in vain   85
From the rude boy or churlish hearted swain
Who beat their stone chinkd forks about the ground
And spread an instant murder all around
Tho oft the anxious maidens tender prayer
Urges the clown their little lives to spare   90
Who sighs while trailing the long rake along
At scenes so cruel and forgets her song
And stays wi love his murder aiming hand
Some ted the puffing winnow down the land
And others following roll them up in heaps   95
While cleanly as a barn door beesom sweeps
The aching drag wi weeds entwind
And swinging rakers toil behind

When the sun stoops to meet the western sky
And noons hot hours have wanderd weary bye   100

They seek an awthorn bush or willow tree
Or stouk or shock where coolest shadows be
Where baskets heapd and unbroached bottles lye
Which dogs in absence watchd with wary eye
To catch their breath awhile and share the boon   105
Which beavering time alows their toil at noon
All gathering sit on stubbs or sheaves the hour
Where scarlet poppys linger still in flower
Stript in his shirt the hot swain drops adown
And close beside him in her unpind gown   110
Next to her favoured swain the maiden steals
Blushing at kindness which her love reveals
Who makes a seat for her of things around
And drops beside her on the naked ground
Wearied wi brambles catching at her gown   115
And pulling nutts from branches pulld adown
By fondling swain the maid wi heaving breast
Upon her lovers shoulder leans at rest
Then from its cool retreat the beer they bring
And hand the stout hooped bottle round the ring   120
Each swain soaks hard—the maiden ere she sips
Shrieks at the bold whasp settling on her lips
That seems determined only hers to greet
As if it fancied they were cherrys sweet
So dog forgoes his sleep awhile or play   125
Springing at frogs that rustling jump away
To watch each morsel that the boon bestows
And wait the bone or crust the shepherd throws
For shepherds are no more of ease possest
But share the harvests labours with the rest   130

When day declines and labour meets repose
The bawling boy his evening journey goes
At toils unwearied call the first and last
He drives his horses to their nights repast
In dewey close or meadow to sojourn   135
And often ventures on his still return
Oer garden pales or orchard walls to hie
When sleeps safe key hath locked up dangers eye
All but the mastiff watching in the dark
Who snuffts and knows him and forbears to bark   140
With fearful haste he climbs each loaded tree
And picks for prizes which the ripest be
Pears plumbs or filberts covered oer in leams
While the pale moon creeps high in peaceful dreams
And oer his harvest theft in jealous light   145
Fills empty shadows with the power to fright
And owlet screaming as it bounces nigh
That from some barn hole pops and hurries bye
Scard at the cat upon her nightly watch
For rats that come for dew upon the thatch   150
He hears the noise and trembling to escape
While every object grows a dismal shape
Drops from the tree in fancys swiftest dread
By ghosts pursued and scampers home to bed
Quick tumbling oer the mossy mouldering wall   155
And looses half his booty in the fall
Where soon as ere the morning opes its eyes
The restless hogs will happen on the prize
And crump adown the mellow and the green
And makes all seem as nothing ne'er had been   160

Amid the broils of harvests weary reign
How sweet the sabbath wakes its rest again
And on each weary mind what rapture dwells
To hear once more its pleasant chiming bells
That from each steeple peeping here and there   165
Murmur a soothing lullaby to care
The shepherd journying on his morning rounds
Pauses awhile to hear their pleasing sounds
While the glad childern free from toils employ
Mimic the ding dong sounds and laugh for joy   170
The fields them selves seem happy to be free
Where insects chatter with unusual glee
While solitude the stubbs and grass among
Appears to muse and listen to the song

In quiet peace awakes the welcomed morn   175
Men tired and childern with their gleaning worn
Weary and stiff lye round their doors the day
To rest themselves with little heart for play
No more keck horns in homestead close resounds
As in their school boy days at hare and hounds   180
Nor running oer the street from wall to wall
With eager shouts at 'cuck and catch the ball'
In calm delight the sabbath wears along
Yet round the cross at noon a tempted throng
Of little younkers with their pence repair   185
To buy the downy plumb and lucious pear
That melt i' th mouth—which gardners never fail
For gains strong impulse to expose for sale
And on the circling cross steps in the sun

Sit when the parson has his sermon done   190
When gardners that against his rules rebell
Come wi their baskets heapd wi fruit to sell
That thither all the season did pursue
Wi mellow goosberrys of every hue
Green ruffs and raspberry reds and drops of gold[1] 195
That makes mouths water often to behold
Sold out to clowns in totts oft deemd too small
Who grudging much the price eat husks and all
Nor leaves a fragment round to cheer the eye
Of searching swine that murmurs hungry bye   200
And currans red and white on cabbage leaves
While childerns fingers itches to be thieves
And black red cherrys shining to the sight
As rich as brandy held before the light
Now these are past he still as sunday comes   205
Sits on the cross wi baskets heapd wi plumbs
And Jenitens streakd apples suggar sweet
Others spice scented ripening wi the wheat
And pears that melt ith' mouth like honey which
He oft declares to make their spirits itch   210
They are so juicy ripe and better still
So rich they een might suck em thro a quill
Here at their leisure gather many a clown
To talk of grain and news about the town
And here the boy wi toils earnd penny comes   215
In hurrying speed to purchase pears or plumbs
And oer the basket hangs wi many a smile
Wi hat in hand to hold his prize the while

[1] These are varieties of gooseberry.

102

Not so the boys that begs for pence in vain
Of deaf eard dames that threat while they complain 220
Who talk of the good dinners they have eat
And wanting more as nothing but consiet
Vowing they ne'er shall throw good pence away
So bids them off and be content wi play
Reaching her rod that hangs the chimney oer   225
And scaring their rude whinings to the door
Who sob aloud and hang their hats adown
To hide their tears and sawn along the town
Venturing wi sullen step his basket nigh
And often dipping a desiring eye   230
Stone hearted dames thrifts errors to believe
Who make their little bellys yearn to thieve
But strong temptation must to fears resign
For close beside the stocks in terror shine
So choaking substitutes for loss of pelf   235
He keeps his longing fingers to himself
And mopes and sits the sabbath hours away
Wi heart too weary and too sad for play
So sundays scenes and leisure passes bye
In rests soft peace and home tranquillity   240
Till monday morning doth its cares pursue
And wakes the harvests busy toils anew

SEPTEMBER

Harvest awakes the morning still
And toils rude groups the valleys fill
Deserted is each cottage hearth
To all life save the crickets mirth
Each burring wheel their sabbath meets   5
Nor walks a gossip in the streets
The bench beneath its eldern bough
Lined oer with grass is empty now
Where black birds caged from out the sun
Would whistle while their mistress spun   10

All haunt the thronged fields still to share
The harvests lingering bounty there
As yet no meddling boys resort
About the streets in idle sport
The butterflye enjoys his hour   15
And flirts unchaced from flower to flower
And humming bees that morning calls
From out the low huts mortar walls
Which passing boy no more controuls
Flye undisturbed about their holes   20
And sparrows in glad chirpings meet
Unpelted in the quiet street

None but imprison'd childern now
Are seen where dames with angry brow
Threaten each younker to his seat   25
That thro' the school door eyes the street
Or from his horn book turns away
To mourn for liberty and play
Loud are the mornings early sounds
That farm and cottage yard surrounds   30
The creaking noise of opening gate
And clanking pumps where boys await
With idle motion to supply
The thirst of cattle crowding bye
The low of cows and bark of dogs   35
And cackling hens and wineing hogs
Swell high—while at the noise awoke
Old goody seeks her milking cloak
And hastens out to milk the cow

And fill the troughs to feed the sow   40
Or seeking old hens laid astray
Or from young chickens drives away
The circling kite that round them flyes
Waiting the chance to seize the prize
Hogs trye thro gates the street to gain   45
And steal into the fields of grain
From nights dull prison comes the duck
Waddling eager thro the muck
Squeezing thro the orchard pales
Where mornings bounty rarely fails   50
Eager gobbling as they pass
Dew worms thro the padded grass
Where blushing apples round and red
Load down the boughs and pat the head
Of longing maid that hither goes   55
To hang on lines the drying cloaths
Who views them oft with tempted eye
And steals one as she passes bye
Where the holly oak so tall
Far oer tops the garden wall   60
That latest blooms for bees provide
Hived on stone benches close beside
The bees their teazing music hum
And threaten war to all that come
Save the old dame whose jealous care   65
Places a trapping bottle there
Filled with mock sweets in whose disguise
The honey loving hornet dies

Upon the dovecotes mossy slates
The piegons coo around their mates 70
And beside the stable wall
Where morns sunbeams early fall
Basking hens in playfull rout
Flap the smoking dust about
In the barn hole sits the cat 75
Watching within the thirsty rat
Who oft at morn its dwelling leaves
To drink the moisture from the eaves
The redbreast with his nimble eye
Dare scarcely stop to catch the flye 80
That tangled in the spiders snare
Mourns in vain for freedom there
The dog beside the threshold lyes
Mocking sleep with half shut eyes
With head crouched down upon his feet 85
Till strangers pass his sunny seat
Then quick he pricks his ears to hark
And bustles up to growl and bark
While boys in fear stop short their song
And sneak on hurrys fears along 90
And beggar creeping like a snail
To make his hungry hopes prevail
Oer the warm heart of charity
Leaves his lame halt and hastens bye

The maid afield now leaves the farm 95
With brimming bottles on her arm
Loitering unseen in narrow lane

107

To be oer took by following swain
Who happy thus her truth to prove
Carrys the load and talks of love 100
Full soon the harvest waggons sound
Rumbling like thunder all around
In ceasless speed the corn to load
Hurrying down the dusty road
While driving boy with eager eye 105
Watches the church clock passing bye
Whose gilt hands glitter in the sun
To see how far the hours have run
Right happly in the breathless day
To see it wearing fast away 110
Yet now and then a sudden shower
Will bring to toil a resting hour
When under sheltering shocks—a crowd
Of merry voices mingle loud
Wearing the short lived boon along 115
With vulgar tale and merry song
Draining with leisures laughing eye
Each welcome bubbling bottle drye
Till peeping suns dry up the rain
Then off they start to toil again 120

Anon the fields are wearing clear
And glad sounds hum in labours ear
When childern halo[1] 'here they come'
And run to meet the harvest home
Stuck thick with boughs and thronged with boys 125
Who mingle loud a merry noise

[1] = halloo.

Glad that the harvests end is nigh
And weary labour nearly bye
Where when they meet the stack thronged yard
Cross bunns or pence their shouts reward   130

Then comes the harvest supper night
Which rustics welcome with delight
When merry game and tiresome tale
And songs increasing with the ale
Their mingled up roar interpose   135
To crown the harvests happy close
While rural mirth that there abides
Laughs till she almost cracks her sides

Now harvests busy hum declines
And labour half its help resigns   140
Boys glad at heart to play return
The shepherds to their peace sojourn
Rush bosomed solitudes among
Which busy toil disturbed so long
The gossip happy all is oer   145
Visits again her neighbours door
For scandals idle tales to dwell
Which harvest had no time to tell
And free from all its sultry strife
Enjoy once more their idle life   150
Some that waining toil reprieves
Thread the forrests sea of leaves
Where the pheasant loves to hide
And the darkest glooms abide

Neath the old oaks mossed and grey 155
Whose shadows seem as old as they
Where time hath many seasons won
Since aught beneath them saw the sun
Within these bramble solitudes
The ragged noisey boy intrudes 160
To gather nuts that ripe and brown
As soon as shook will patter down
Thus harvest ends its busy reign
And leaves the fields their peace again
Where autumns shadows idly muse 165
And tinge the trees with many hues
Amid whose scenes I'm feign to dwell
And sing of what I love so well
But hollow winds and tumbling floods
And humming showers and moaning woods 170
All startle into sudden strife
And wake a mighty lay to life
Making amid their strains divine
All songs in vain so mean as mine

OCTOBER

Nature now spreads around in dreary hue
A pall to cover all that summer knew
Yet in the poets solitary way
Some pleasing objects for his praise delay
Somthing that makes him pause and turn again   5
As every trifle will his eye detain
The free horse rustling thro the stubble field
And cows at lare in rushes half conscealed
With groups of restless sheep who feed their fill
Oer cleard fields rambling where so ere they will   10

111

The geese flock gabbling in the splashy fields
And quacking ducks in pondweeds half conseald
Or seeking worms along the homclose sward
Right glad of freedom from the prison yard
While every cart rut dribbles its low tide   15
And every hollow splashy sports provide
The hedger stopping gaps amid the leaves
That oer his head in every color weaves
The milk maid stepping with a timid look
From stone to stone across the brimming brook   20
The cotter journying wi his noisey swine
Along the wood ride where the brambles twine
Shaking from dinted cups the acorns brown
And from the hedges red awes dashing down
And nutters rustling in the yellow woods   25
Still scare the wild things from their solitudes
And squirrels secret toils oer winter dreams
Picking the brown nuts from the yellow leams
And hunters from the thickets avenue
In scarlet jackets startling on the view   30
Skiming a moment oer the russet plain
Then hiding in the colord woods again
The ploping guns sharp momentary shock
Which eccho bustles from her cave to mock
The inly pleased tho solitary boy   35
Journeying and muttering oer his dreams of joy
Haunting the hedges for the wilding fruit
Of sloe or black berry just as fancys suit
The sticking groups in many a ragged set
Brushing the woods their harmless loads to get   40

And gipseys camps in some snug shelterd nook
Where old lane hedges like the pasture brook
Run crooking as they will by wood and dell
In such lone spots these wild wood roamers dwell
On commons where no farmers claims appear   45
Nor tyrant justice rides to interfere
Such the abodes neath hedge or spreading oak
And but discoverd by its curling smoak
Puffing and peeping up as wills the breeze
Between the branches of the colord trees   50
Such are the pictures that october yields
To please the poet as he walks the fields
While nature like fair woman in decay
Which pale consumption hourly wastes away
Upon her waining features pale and chill   55
Wears dreams of beauty that seem lovely still
Among the heath furze still delights to dwell
Quaking as if with cold the harvest bell
The mushroom buttons each moist morning brings
Like spots of snow in the green tawney rings   60
And fuzz balls swelld like bladders in the grass
Which oft the merry laughing milking lass
Will stoop to gather in her sportive airs
And slive in mimickd fondness unawares
To smut the brown cheek of the teazing swain   65
With the black powder which their balls contain
Who feigns offence at first that love may speed
Then claims a kiss to recompence the deed
The singing maid in fancy ever gay
Loitering along the mornings dripping way   70

With wicker basket swinging on her arm
Searching the hedges of home close or farm
Where brashy eldern trees to autumn fade
Wild shines the hedge in autumns gay parade
The glossy berrys picturesquely weaves   75
Their swathy bunches mid the yellow leaves
Where the pert sparrow stains his little bill
And tutling robin picks his meals at will
Black ripening to the wan suns misty ray
Here the industrious hus wives wend their way   80
Pulling the brittle branches carefull down
And hawking loads of berrys to the town
While village dames as they get ripe and fine
Repair to pluck them for their 'eldern wine'
That bottld up becomes a rousing charm   85
To kindle winters icy bosom warm
That wi its merry partner nut brown beer
Makes up the peasants christmass keeping cheer

Like to a painted map the landscape lies
And wild above shine the cloud thronged skies   90
The flying clouds urged on in swiftest pace
Like living things as if they runned a race
The winds that oer each coming tempest broods
Waking like spirits in their startling moods
Fluttering the sear leaves on the blackning lea   95
That litters under every fading tree
And pausing oft as falls the patting rain
Then gathering strength and twirling them again
Till drops the sudden calm—the hurried mill

Is stopt at once and every noise is still 100
The startld stockdove hurried wizzing bye
As the still hawk hangs oer him in the sky
Crows from the oak trees quawking as they spring
Dashing the acorns down wi beating wing
Waking the woodlands sleep in noises low 105
Patting the crimpt brakes withering brown below
The starnel crowds that dim the muddy light
And puddock circling round its lazy flight
Round the wild sweeing wood in motion slow
Before it perches on the oaks below 110
And hugh black beetles revelling alone
In the dull evening with their heavy drone
Buzzing from barn door straw and hovel sides
Where fodderd cattle from the night abides
These pictures linger thro the shortning day 115
And cheer the lone bards mellancholy way
Till surly Winter comes with biting breath
And strips the woods and numbs the scene with death
Then all is still oer wood and field and plain
As nought had been and nought would be again 120

NOVEMBER

The village sleeps in mist from morn till noon
And if the sun wades thro tis wi a face
Beamless and pale and round as if the moon
When done the journey of its nightly race
Had found him sleeping and supplyd his place   5
For days the shepherds in the fields may be
Nor mark a patch of sky—blind fold they trace
The plains that seem wi out a bush or tree
Wistling aloud by guess to flocks they cannot see

The timid hare seems half its fears to loose   10
Crouching and sleeping neath its grassy lare

116

And scarcly startles tho the shepherd goes
Close by its home and dogs are barking there
The wild colt only turns around to stare
At passers bye then naps his hide again   15
And moody crows beside the road forbeer[1]
To flye tho pelted by the passing swain
Thus day seems turned to night and trys to wake in
    vain

The Owlet leaves her hiding place at noon
And flaps her grey wings in the doubting light   20
The hoarse jay screams to see her out so soon
And small birds chirp and startle with affright
Much doth it scare the superstitious wight
Who dreams of sorry luck and sore dismay
While cow boys think the day a dream of night   25
And oft grow fearful on their lonly way
Who fancy ghosts may wake and leave their graves by
    day

The cleanly maiden thro the village streets
In pattens clicks down causways never drye
While eaves above head drops—where oft she meets   30
The school boy leering on wi mischiefs eye
Trying to splash her as he hurrys bye
While swains afield returning to their ploughs
Their passing aid wi gentle speech apply
And much loves rapture thrills when she alows   35
Their help wi offerd hand to lead her oer the sloughs

[1] = forbear.

117

The hedger soakd wi the dull weather chops
On at his toils which scarcly keeps him warm
And every stroke he takes large swarms of drops
Patter about him like an april storm   40
The sticking dame wi cloak upon her arm
To guard against a storm walks the wet leas
Of willow groves or hedges round the farm
Picking up aught her splashy wanderings sees
Dead sticks the sudden winds have shook from off the
    trees   45

The boy that scareth from the spirey wheat
The mellancholy crow—quakes while he weaves
Beneath the ivey tree a hut and seat
Of rustling flags and sedges tyd in sheaves
Or from nigh stubble shocks a shelter thieves   50
There he doth dithering sit or entertain
His leisure hours down hedges lost to leaves
While spying nests where he spring eggs hath taen
He wishes in his heart twas summer time again

And oft he'll clamber up a sweeing tree   55
To see the scarlet hunter hurry bye
And feign[1] woud in their merry uproar be
But sullen labour hath its tethering tye
Crows swop around and some on bushes nigh
Watch for a chance when ere he turns away   60
To settle down their hunger to supply
From morn to eve his toil demands his stay
Save now and then an hour which leisure steals for play

---

[1] = fain

Gaunt grey hounds now their coursing sports impart
Wi long legs stretchd on tip toe for the chase   65
And short loose ear and eye upon the start
Swift as the wind their motions they unlace
When bobs the hare up from her hiding place
Who in its furry coat of fallow stain
Squats on the lands or wi a dodging pace   70
Tryes its old coverts of wood grass to gain
And oft by cunning ways makes all their speed in vain

Dull for a time the slumbering weather flings
Its murky prison round then winds wake loud
Wi sudden start the once still forest sings   75
Winters returning song cloud races cloud
And the orison throws away its shrowd
And sweeps its stretching circle from the eye
Storm upon storm in quick succession crowd
And oer the samness of the purple skye   80
Heaven paints its wild irregularity

The shepherd oft foretells by simple ways
The weathers change that will ere long prevail
He marks the dull ass that grows wild and brays
And sees the old cows gad adown the vale   85
A summer race and snuff the coming gale
The old dame sees her cat wi fears alarm
Play hurly burly races wi its tale
And while she stops her wheel her hands to warm
She rubs her shooting corns and prophecys a storm   90

Morts are the signs—the stone hid toad will croak
And gobbling turkey cock wi noises vile
Dropping his snout as flaming as a cloak
Loose as a red rag oer his beak the while
Urging the dame to turn her round and smile   95
To see his uncooth pride her cloaths attack
Sidling wi wings hung down in vapourey broil
And feathers ruffld up while oer his back
His tail spreads like a fan cross wavd wi bars of black

The hog sturts round the stye and champs the straw   100
And bolts about as if a dog was bye
The steer will cease its gulping cud to chew
And toss his head wi wild and startld eye
At windshook straws—the geese will noise and flye
Like wild ones to the pond—wi matted mane   105
The cart horse squeals and kicks his partner nigh
While leaning oer his fork the foddering swain
The uproar marks around and dreams of wind and rain

And quick it comes among the forest oaks
Wi sobbing ebbs and uproar gathering high   110
The scard hoarse raven on its cradle croaks
And stock dove flocks in startld terrors flye
While the blue hawk hangs oer them in the skye
The shepherd happy when the day is done
Hastes to his evening fire his cloaths to dry   115
And forrester crouchd down the storm to shun
Scarce hears amid the strife the poachers muttering gun

The ploughman hears the sudden storm begin
And hies for shelter from his naked toil
Buttoning his doublet closer to his chin   120
He speeds him hasty oer the elting soil
While clouds above him in wild fury boil
And winds drive heavily the beating rain
He turns his back to catch his breath awhile
Then ekes his speed and faces it again   125
To seek the shepherds hut beside the rushy plain

Oft stripping cottages and barns of thack
Where startld farmer garnerd up his grain
And wheat and bean and oat and barley stack
Leaving them open to the beating rain   130
The husbandman grieves oer his loss in vain
And sparrows mourn their night nests spoild and bare
The thackers they resume their toils again
And stubbornly the tall red ladders bare
While to oerweight the wind they hang old harrows
   there   135

Thus wears the month along in checkerd moods
Sunshine and shadow tempests loud and calms
One hour dyes silent oer the sleepy woods
The next wakes loud with unexpected storms
A dreary nakedness the field deforms   140
Yet many rural sounds and rural sights
Live in the village still about the farms
Where toils rude uproar hums from morn till night
Noises in which the ear of industry delights:

Hoarse noise of field-free bull that strides ahead   145
Of the tail switching herd to feed again
The barking mastiff from his kennel bed
Urging his teazing noise at passing swain
The jostling rumble of the sturting wain
From the farm yard where freedoms chance to wait 150
The turkey drops his snout—and geese in vain
Noise at the signal of the opening gate
Then from the clowns whip flyes and finds the chance
   too late

The pigeon wi its breast of many hues
That spangles to the sun turns round and round   155
About his timid sidling mate and croos
Upon the cottage ridge where oer their heads
The puddock sails oft swopping oer the pen
Where timid chickens from their parent stray
That skulk and scutter neath her wings agen   160
Nor peeps no more till they have saild away[1]

Such rural sounds the mornings tongue renews
And rural sights swarm on the rustics eye
The billy goat shakes from his beard the dews
And jumps the wall wi carting teams to hie   165
Upon the barn rig at their freedom flye
The spotted guiney fowl—hogs in the stye
Agen the door in rooting whinings stand
The freed colt drops his head and gallops bye
The boy that holds a scuttle in his hand   170
Prefering unto toil the commons rushy land

[1] Defective stanza.

NOVEMBER

At length the noise of busy toil is still
And industry awhile her care forgoes
When winter comes in earnest to fulfill
Her yearly task at bleak novembers close   175
And stops the plough and hides the field in snows
When frost locks up the streams in chill delay
And mellows on the hedge the purple sloes
For little birds—then toil hath time for play
And nought but threshers flails awake the dreary day 180

DECEMBER

CHRISTMASS

Christmass is come and every hearth
Makes room to give him welcome now
Een want will dry its tears in mirth
And crown him wi a holly bough
Tho tramping neath a winter sky   5
Oer snow track paths and ryhmey[1] stiles
The hus wife sets her spining bye
And bids him welcome wi her smiles

[1] = rimy.

Each house is swept the day before
And windows stuck wi evergreens   10
The snow is beesomd from the door
And comfort crowns the cottage scenes
Gilt holly wi its thorny pricks
And yew and box wi berrys small
These deck the unusd candlesticks   15
And pictures hanging by the wall

Neighbours resume their anual cheer
Wishing wi smiles and spirits high
Glad christmass and a happy new year
To every morning passer bye   20
Milk maids their christmass journeys go
Accompanyd wi favourd swain
And childern pace the crumping snow
To taste their grannys cake again

Hung wi the ivys veining bough   25
The ash trees round the cottage farm
Are often stript of branches now
The cotters christmass hearth to warm
He swings and twists his hazel band
And lops them off wi sharpend hook   30
And oft brings ivy in his hand
To decorate his chimney nook

Old winter whipes his icles bye
And warms his fingers till he smiles
Where cottage hearths are blazing high   35
And labour resteth from his toils

125

Wi merry mirth beguiling care
Old customs keeping wi the day
Friends meet their christmass cheer to share
And pass it in a harmless way   40

Old customs O I love the sound
However simple they may be
What ere wi time has sanction found
Is welcome and is dear to me
Pride grows above simplicity   45
And spurns it from her haughty mind
And soon the poets song will be
The only refuge they can find

The shepherd now no more afraid
Since custom doth the chance bestow   50
Starts up to kiss the giggling maid
Beneath the branch of mizzletoe
That neath each cottage beam is seen
Wi pearl-like-berrys shining gay
The shadow still of what hath been   55
Which fashion yearly fades away

And singers too a merry throng
At early morn wi simple skill
Yet imitate the angels song
And chant their christmass ditty still   60
And mid the storm that dies and swells
By fits—in humings softly steals
The music of the village bells
Ringing round their merry peals

And when its past a merry crew   65
Bedeckt in masks and ribbons gay
The 'Morrice dance' their sports renew
And act their winter evening play
The clown-turnd-kings for penny praise
Storm wi the actors strut and swell   70
And harlequin a laugh to raise
Wears his hump back and tinkling bell

And oft for pence and spicy ale
Wi winter nosgays pind before
The wassail singer tells her tale   75
And drawls her christmass carrols oer
The prentice boy wi ruddy face
And ryhme[1] bepowderd dancing locks
From door to door wi happy pace
Runs round to claim his 'christmass box'   80

The block behind the fire is put
To sanction customs old desires
And many a faggots bands are cut
For the old farmers christmass fires
Where loud tongd gladness joins the throng 85
And winter meets the warmth of may
Feeling by times the heat too strong
And rubs his shins and draws away

While snows the window panes bedim
The fire curls up a sunny charm   90
Where creaming oer the pitchers rim
The flowering ale is set to warm

[1] = rime.

Mirth full of joy as summer bees
Sits there its pleasures to impart
While childern tween their parents knees   95
Sing scraps of carrols oer by heart

And some to view the winter weathers
Climb up the window seat wi glee
Likening the snow to falling feathers
In fancys infant extacy   100
Laughing wi superstitions love
Oer visions wild that youth supplyes
Of people pulling geese above
And keeping christmass in the skyes

As tho the homstead trees were drest   105
In lieu of snow wi dancing leaves
As tho the sun dryd martins nest
Instead of icles hung the eaves
The childern hail the happy day
As if the snow was april grass   110
And pleasd as neath the warmth of may
Sport oer the water froze to glass

Thou day of happy sound and mirth
That long wi childish memory stays
How blest around the cottage hearth   115
I met thee in my boyish days
Harping wi raptures dreaming joys
Oer presents that thy coming found
The welcome sight of little toys
The christmass gifts of commers round   120

The wooden horse wi arching head
Drawn upon wheels around the room
The gilded coach of ginger bread
And many colord sugar plumb
Gilt coverd books for pictures sought 125
Or storys childhood loves to tell
Wi many a urgent promise bought
To get tomorrows lesson well

And many a thing a minutes sport
Left broken on the sanded floor 130
When we woud leave our play and court
Our parents promises for more
Tho manhood bids such raptures dye
And throws such toys away as vain
Yet memory loves to turn her eye 135
And talk such pleasures oer again

Around the glowing hearth at night
The harmless laugh and winter tale
Goes round—while parting friends delight
To toast each other oer their ale 140
The cotter oft wi quiet zeal
Will musing oer his bible lean
While in the dark the lovers steal
To kiss and toy behind the screen

The yule cake dotted thick wi plumbs 145
Is on each supper table found
And cats look up for falling crumbs
Which greedy childern litter round

And hus wifes sage stuffd seasond chine
Long hung in chimney nook to drye   150
And boiling eldern berry wine
To drink the christmass eves 'good bye'

JULY (SECOND VERSION)

July the month of summers prime
Again resumes her busy time
Scythes tinkle in each grassy dell
Where solitude was wont to dwell
And meadows they are mad with noise   5
Of laughing maids and shouting boys
Making up the withering hay
With merry hearts as light as play
The very insects on the ground
So nimbly bustle all around   10
Among the grass or dusty soil
They seem partakers in the toil
The very landscap reels with life
While mid the busy stir and strife
Of industry the shepherd still   15
Enjoys his summer dreams at will
Bent oer his hook or listless laid
Beneath the pastures willow shade
Whose foliage shines so cool and grey
Amid the sultry hues of day   20
As if the mornings misty veil
Yet lingered in their shadows pale
Or lolling in a musing mood
On mounds where saxon castles stood
Upon whose deeply buried walls   25
The ivyed oaks dark shadow falls
Oft picking up with wondering gaze
Some little thing of other days

131

Saved from the wreck of time—as beads
Or broken pots among the weeds   30
Of curious shapes—and many a stone
Of roman pavements thickly sown
Oft hoping as he searches round
That buried riches may be found
Tho search as often as he will   35
His hopes are dissapointed still
And marking oft upon his seat
The insect world beneath his feet
In busy motion here and there
Like visitors to feast or fair   40
Some climbing up the rushes stem
A steeples height or more to them
With speed that sees no fear to drop
Till perched upon its spirey top
Where they awhile the view survey   45
Then prune their wings and flit away
Others journying too and fro
Throng the grassy woods below
Musing as if they felt and knew
The pleasant scenes they wandered thro   50
Where each bent round them seems to be
A hugh and massive timber tree
While pismires from their castles come
In crowds to seek the litterd crumb
Which he on purpose drops that they   55
May hawl the heavy loads away
Shaping the while their dark employs
To his own visionary joys
Picturing such a life as theirs
As free from summers sweating cares   60
And inly wishing that his own

Coud meet with joys so thickly sown
He thinks sport all that they pursue
And play the all they have to do
The cowboy still cuts short the day   65
Mingling mischief with his play
Oft in the pond with weeds oer grown
Hurling quick the plashing stone
To cheat his dog who watching lies
And instant plunges for the prize   70
And tho each effort proves as vain
He shakes his coat and dives again
Till wearied with the fruitless play
Then drops his tail and sneaks away
Nor longer heeds the bawling boy   75
Who seeks new sports with added joy
And on some banks oer hanging brow
Beats the whasps nest with a bough
Till armys from the hole appear
And threaten vengance in his ear   80
With such determined hue and cry
As makes the bold besiegers flye
Elsewhere fresh mischief to renew
And still his teazing sports pursue
Pelting with excessive glee   85
The squirrel on the wood land tree
Who nimbles round from grain to grain
And cocks his tail and peeps again
Half pleased as if he thought the fray
Which mischief made was meant for play   90
Till scared and startled into flight
He instant hurries out of sight
Thus he his leisure hour employs
And feeds on busy meddling joys

133

While in the willow shaded pool 95
His cattle stand their hides to cool

Loud is the summers busy song
The smallest breeze can find a tongue
Where insects of each tiney size
Grow teazing with their melodys 100
Till noon burns with its blistering breath
Around and day dyes still as death
The busy noise of man and brute
Is on a sudden lost and mute
The cuckoo singing as she flies 105
No more to mocking boy replys
Even the brook that leaps along
Seems weary of its bubbling song
And so soft its waters creep
Tired silence sinks in sounder sleep 110
The cricket on its banks is dumb
The very flies forget to hum
And save the waggon rocking round
The lanscape sleeps without a sound
The breeze is stopt the lazy bough 115
Hath not a leaf that dances now
The totter grass upon the hill
And spiders threads are standing still
The feathers dropt from more hens wing
Which to the waters surface cling 120
Are stedfast and as heavy seem
As stones beneath them in the stream
Hawkweeds and Groundsells fanning downs
Unruffled keep their seedy crowns
And in the oven heated air 125
Not one light thing is floating there

—Save that to the earnest eye
The restless heat seems twittering bye
Noon swoons beneath the heat it made
And flowers een wither in the shade   130
Untill the sun slopes in the west
Like weary traveler glad to rest
On pillard¹ clouds of many hues
Then natures voice its joy renews
And checkerd field and grassy plain   135
Hum with their summer songs again
A requiem to the days decline
Whose setting sun beams cooly shine
As welcome to days feeble powers
As evening dews on thirsty flowers   140

Now to the pleasant pasture dells
Where hay from closes sweetly smells
Adown the pathways narrow lane
The milking maiden hies again
With scraps of ballads never dumb   145
And rosey cheeks of happy bloom
Tanned brown by sumers rude embrace
That adds new beautys to her face
And red lips never paled with sighs
And flowing hair and laughing eyes   150
That oer full many a heart prevailed
And swelling bosom loosly veiled
White as the love it harbours there
Unsullied with the taints of care
The mower gives his labour oer   155
And on his bench beside the door
Sits down to see his childern play
Or smokes his leisure hour away

¹ = pillowed.

135

JULY (SECOND VERSION)

While from her cage the black bird sings
That on the wood bine arbour hings   160
And all with happy joys recieve
The quiet of a summers eve

a, on the.
ach *v.*, ache.
agen, *adv.*, again.
anker *v.*, hanker.
ant *v.*, ain't, are not.
arum *n.*, lords and ladies, cuckoopint, *Arum maculatum*.
awe *n.*, haw.
awthorn *n.*, hawthorn.

baffles *n. pl.*, leggings, gaiters.
balk, bauk, baulk *n.*, strip of grass between ploughed lands.
bare *v.*, bear.
barkman *n.*, man who collects oak-bark for making tannic acid.
beaver *n.*, hat, originally of beaver fur.
be(a)vering time *n.*, time for a break for refreshment.
beesom *v.*, sweep.
beesom *n.*, broom made of twigs.
beetle *n.*, heavy mallet used for driving wedges.

bent *n.*, twig; coarse grass.
benty *adj.*, coarse.
Bess in her bravery *n.*, probably the double-flowered garden daisy with a mass of crimson-tipped white petals.
bird boy *n.*, boy who frightens birds from the corn.
black thorn *n.*, sloe, *Prunus spinosa*.
bleb, blob, *see* **horse bleb**.
blood wall *n.*, dark, double wall-flower.
blue cap *n.*, blue corn-flower, *Centaurea cyanus*.
blue hawk *n.*, (*a*) peregrine, *Falco peregrinus* or (*b*) hen harrier, *Circus cyaneus*.
bolt *v.*, appear or move suddenly.
boon *n.*, break from toil.
bottle brush *n.*, popular name for horse-tail, mare's tail.
brake *v.*, break.
brashy *adj.*, delicate.
brig *n.*, bridge.

briony *n.*, mandrake, *Bryonia dioica*.

brouze *v.*, browse.

bum barrel *n.*, long-tailed tit, *Aegithalos caudatus*.

bunting *n.*, corn bunting, *Emberiza calandra*.

burdock *n.*, coarse weed, *Arctium lappa*.

burr *v.*, purr, hum, drone.

cabbage rose *n.*, the Provins rose, *Rosa centifolia*.

cag *n.*, small cask, keg, basket.

carless *adj.*, careless.

carlock *n.*, charlock, *Sinapis arvensis*.

charleses wain *n.*, the seven bright stars of the Plough.

childern *n. pl.*, children.

chimble *v.*, nibble, chew.

chine *n.*, joint of meat consisting of the whole or part of the backbone of an animal, with the adjoining flesh.

christmass box *n.*, gift presented at Christmas or on the next day, Boxing Day.

clipping pink *n.*, common garden carnation.

clipping posey *n.*, nosegays presented to sheepshearers, which were frequently sprinkled with snuff or pepper to excite the mirth of the company by the unexpected titillation and sneezing they occasion.

clipping tide *n.*, shearing time.

close *n.*, enclosed field, especially for pasturing cattle.

clown *n.*, rustic, yokel, labourer.

cocks stride *n.*, short stride, used of the time by which the days lengthen in spring.

colom *n.*, column.

colter *n.*, coulter.

columbine *n.*, *Aquilegia vulgaris*.

cotter *n.*, cottager.

coying *part.*, decoying, misleading.

crab *n.*, crab-apple, *Malus sylvestris*.

crank *v.*, sing dolefully; croak.

crimp(le) *v.*, ripple; ruffle; wrinkle.

crimpling *adj*., hobbling; limping; moving with pain and stiffness.

crimpt *adj*., wrinkled.

crizzle *v*., roughen, as water when it begins to freeze.

croo *v*., make a noise like a dove or pigeon.

croodle *v*., shrink from cold.

crooking *adj*., turning; bending; twisting.

cross bunn *n*., spicy bun with a cross marked on it, traditionally sold on Good Friday.

crowflower *n*., buttercup, *Ranunculus arvensis*.

crow-pot-stone *n*., fossil shell, gryphite.

crump *v*., crunch.

cuck and catch *v*., game played with cucking balls, made of flowers, esp. cowslips.

cucking ball *n*., ball of flowers for throwing in May games.

curnel *n*., kernel.

curran *n*., currant.

custom *adj*., customary.

damsin *n*., damson.

daw *n*., jackdaw.

dengle *v*., dangle.

dinted *adj*., dented.

dither *v*., tremble with cold.

douse *v*., dowse, drench, soak.

drabble *v*., trail along in the mud.

drops of gold *n. pl*., variety of gooseberry or plum.

duck under water *n*., game in which the players run, two by two, in rapid succession under a handkerchief held up by two others.

edding *n*., headland, strip of grass at the end of a field where the plough turns.

eke *v*., increase.

eldern *n*., elder tree, *Sambucus nigra*.

elting *adj*., soft, moist, damp (of soil new-ploughed).

feign *v*., fain.

firdale *n*., fir tree.

fire tail *n*., redstart, *Phoenicurus phoenicurus*.

flirt *v*., flit, flutter.

flitter *v*., flutter.

flower *n*., flour.

flurt *v*., var. of **flirt**.

follow *adj.*, fallow.
footbrig *n.*, foot-bridge.
forbeer *v.*, forbear.
fore *n.*, bank, edge or brink of pool.
fore horse *n.*, leading horse of a plough team.
frail *n.*, flail.
fret *v.*, thaw.
frumity *n.*, frumenty, a dish made of hulled wheat boiled in milk and seasoned.

gad *n.*, gad-fly.
gadding *part.*, moving restlessly.
gangling *part.*, jangling.
gears *n. pl.*, harness.
gingling *part.*, jingling.
gleg *v.*, peep.
glib *adj.*, smooth, slippery.
golden crested wren *n.*, goldcrest, *Regulus regulus*.
goody *n.*, old woman.
green ruffs *n. pl.*, variety of gooseberry.
grinning *adj.*, of stitches that are so wide asunder and deeply set in that they look like teeth, used by Clare of icicles.
grizzle *v.*, darken, turn lowering, look dark and threatening.

halo, hallow *v.*, halloo.
hant *n.*, haunt.
hare & hounds *n.*, game in which the 'hounds' pursue the 'hare' after givng him a start.
harvest home *n.*, the harvest ceremony. Clare gives a fuller description at A31–130/1:
'Oer all the horses backs white sheets were spread
And light blue ribbons hung at eithers head
And on the shockers rakes that went behind
Silk hankerchiefs hung flopping in the wind
And boys that rode before stuck rush tyd platts
Of ash key branches in their rusty hats'
head ache *n.*, common poppy, *Papaver rhoeas*.
heads *n. pl.*, 'to pick up heads', side of an English coin showing the monarch's head.
hen bane *n.*, *Hysoscyamus niger*.

hidy holes *n.*, hiding places.

higgle *v.*, work at anything slowly and laboriously.

high *v.*, hie, go somewhere.

hilo *n.*, high-low; boot covering the ankles.

hing *v.*, hang.

hodge *n.*, typical English agricultural labourer.

holly oak *n.*, hollyhock, *Malva rosea*.

horehound cake *n.*, made from the herb white horehound, *Marrubium vulgare*, used medicinally since Egyptian times to treat numerous ailments.

horse bleb *n.*, marsh-marigold, *Caltha palustris*.

horse blob *n.*, var. of **horse bleb**.

horse tail *n.*, cryptogamous plant of genus *Equisetum* with hollow jointed stem.

hors(e)bee *n.*, (*a*) horse bot-fly or (*b*) cleg.

hovel *n.*, rough shelter for cattle.

hugh *adj.*, huge.

hulk *n.*, temporary shelter used by shepherds in the lambing season.

hurd *v.*, hoard, store.

hussle *v.*, toss. Cf. 'pitch and hussel'.

i th, ith', in the.

ic(k)le *n.*, icicle.

iron weed *n.*, knapweed, *Centaurea nigra*.

Jack a lanthorn *n.*, *Ignus fatuus*, will-o'-the-wisp.

jelt *v.*, throw, fling.

Jeniten *n.*, jenneting, early sweet apple.

jiant *n.*, giant.

jiliflower *n.*, gilliflower, wall-flower, *Cheiranthus cheiri*.

jilt *v.*, throw, fling.

John go bed at noon *n.*, scarlet pimpernel, *Anagallis arvensis*.

jumping flye *n.*, turnip fly.

keck *n.*, dried stalk of cow parsley or similar plants.

keck horn *n.*, horn made from kecks.

kee *n.*, key.

keetle *n.*, kettle.

knap *v.*, bite, nibble.

knat *n.*, gnat.

knopweed *n.*, knapweed.

lader *n.*, ladder.

lads love *n.*, southernwood, *Artemisia abrotanum*.

lair *v.*, find a safe place.

land *n.*, arable division of a furlong in an open field.

lanthorn *n.*, lantern.

lap *v.*, wrap, fold.

lare *n.*, lair.

larkheel *n.*, larkspur, *Delphinium ambiguum*.

lathy *adj.*, thin, slender, as a lath of wood.

leam *n.*, husk.

linnet *n.*, furze or goss lark, *Acanthis cannabina*.

loath *adj.*, loth.

lob *v.*, lope, walk heavily.

London tuft *n.*, London pride, *Saxifraga umbrosa*.

loose *v.*, lose.

lump *v.*, thump, beat, thresh.

lushing *adj.*, abundant, luxuriant.

mallow *n.*, *Malva sylvestris*.

martin *n.*, house martin, *Delichon urbica*.

maul *v.*, drag along wearily, plod with difficulty.

mavis thrush *n.*, mistle thrush or storm cock, *Turdus viscivorous*.

mawking thorn *n.*, thorn tied to the last cow brought on to the pasture on May Day and therefore a disgrace to the milk-maid.

meadow sorrel *n.*, common sorrel, *Rumex acetosa*. Also known as 'sour grass' because of the sharp taste of the leaves which are sometimes added to salads.

midgeon *n.*, midge, gnat.

moil *v.*, toil, labour.

moment *adj.*, momentary.

mong *prep.*, among.

monkshood *n.*, poisonous plant, *Aconitum napelius*.

more hen *n.*, moorhen, *Gallinula chloropus*.

mores, more is.

mort *n.*, lot, large number.

motling *part.*, mottling, speckled, variegated.

mozzld, **mozzling** *adj.*, of rubbed indistinct pattern, mottled, of various colours.

nap *v.*, bite, nibble.

nauntle *v.*, elevate, hold oneself erect, raise.

newsings *n. pl.*, news, gossip, tidings.

night hawk *n.*, fern owl, nightjar, *Caprimulgus europaeus*.

nimble *v.*, move quickly, dart.

nookey *adj.*, with nooks or corners.

nott *n.*, knot.

oddling *adj.*, odd; scattered.

oggle *n.*, ogle.

orison *n.*, horizon.

pail, **pale** *n.*, paling.

pansion *n.*, brown earthenware vessel.

patten *n.*, overshoe with wooden sole on iron ring for raising wearer's shoes out of the mud.

peep *n.*, single blossom of flowers growing in a cluster.

piegon *n.*, pigeon.

pillard *adj.*, pillowed.

pimpernel *n.*, scarlet pimpernel, *Anagallis arvensis*, also known as shepherd's or poor man's weather-glass.

pinfold *n.*, sheep-fold.

pismire *n.*, ant, *Leontodon taraxacum*.

pitch & toss *n.*, game of skill and chance in which coins are pitched at a mark and then tossed.

plad *n.*, plaid.

plash *v.*, splash.

platt *n.*, plot, flat stretch of ground.

poddle *n.*, toddle.

pooty *n.*, land snail, *Cepaea nemoralis*.

prentice *n.*, apprentice.

princifeather *n.*, lilac, *Syringa vulgaris*.

prune *v.*, preen (of a bird's feathers), still used in this sense in Helpston today.

puddock *n.*, kite, *Milvus milvus*, but also used by Clare of the buzzard.

pudgy *adj.*, sticky, muddy, full of puddles.

pye *n.*, magpie.

quail *n.*, *Coturnix coturnix*.

quawk *v.*, squawk, caw.

quick *n.*, young hawthorn plant.

rail *n.*, landrail, corncrake.

ramping *adj.*, romping, wildly spreading.

rap *v.*, wrap.

raspberry reds *n. pl.*, wild raspberry, *Rubus idaeus*.

red cap *n.*, goldfinch, *Carduelis carduelis*.

reed shaw *n.*, reed bed.

reek *v.*, smoke, steam.

rid *p.p.*, rode.

rig *n.*, ridge.

ring dove *n.*, woodpigeon, *Columba palumbus*.

rock *v.*, roll, sway, walk unsteadily.

rooting *adj.*, taking root.

ruffs *see* **green ruffs**.

sawn *v.*, saunter, loiter, dally.

scape, *n.*, escape.

scrat *v.*, scratch.

scutter *v.*, scuttle, run briskly.

scuttle *n.*, shallow wooden or wicker basket.

seer *adj.*, sear.

seven stars *n. pl.*, the Plough.

shepherd's weather-glass *see* **pimpernel**.

shill *adj.*, shrill.

shocker *n.*, person who ties up the sheaves.

shock *n.*, sheaf.

shoy *adj.*, shy.

shoyness *n.*, shyness.

sicken *v.*, move in sickly fashion.

sidle *v.*, saunter, meander.

sifter *n.*, kitchen shovel, fire shovel.

sile *v.*, glide, fleet past.

sissars *n. pl.*, scissors.

skait *v.*, skate.

slive *v.*, slide, slip, sneak about.

smell smock *n.*, dialect name for several plants, esp. cuckoo-flower or ladysmock, *Cardamine pratensis*.

snive *v.*, swarm, abound.

snu(f)ft *v.*, snuff, sniff.

soodle *v.*, dawdle, idle, stroll, saunter.

sour grass *see* **meadow sorrel**.

spirey *adj.*, pointing and tapering like a spire.

sputter *v.*, splutter.

starnel *n.*, starling.

sticking *adj.*, gathering wood or sticks for fire wood.

streak *v.*, stretch.

144

stroying *part*., destroying.

strunt *adj*., stunted, cut short, up-turned (of a bird's tail).

struttle *n*., stickleback, *Gasterostens aculeatus*.

stulp *n*., stump of a tree.

stunt *adj*., steep, abrupt.

sturnel *n*., starling.

sturt *v*., startle, disturb, move suddenly.

style *n*., stile.

sue *v*., sew.

sutty *adj*., sooty.

swaily *adj*., shady, cool.

swathy *adj*., swarthy.

swee *v*., sway, swing.

sweet briar *n*., *Rosa rubiginosa*.

swive *v*., OE swifan, to move in a course, sweep: ME to copulate. Seems here to have the meaning 'to bunch'.

swop *v*., swoop, pounce, as a bird on its prey.

taen *p.p*., taken.

taw *n*., child's marble.

tazzel *n*., tassle.

thack *n*., thatch.

thacker *n*., thatcher.

then *conj*., than.

throngd *adj*., thronged, busy.

tongd *adj*., tongued.

tithman *n*., titheman, one who marks each tenth sheaf for the parson's tithe.

totter grass *n*., quaking-grass, *Briza media*.

tray *n*., hurdle or fence for confining sheep.

truck *v*., possibly variant for 'tuck'.

tuggle *v*., tug, pull.

tutle *v*., tootle.

twitch *n*., common couch grass, *Agropyron repens*.

twitter *v*., flicker, glitter, squeak.

unbrichd *adj*., unbreeched.

unbrinkd *adj*., hat with no brim to protect the face.

unconcous *adj*., uncon-scious.

velted *adj*., felted.

waffle *v*., yap, bark.

wallet *n*., bag.

wash pit (**pot**) *n*., dipping pool for the sheep.

way *n*., whey.

weal *v.*, raise marks on the skin with a whip.

weel *n.*, wheel.

while *conj.*, until.

whittleseas reed wooded mere *n.*, Whittlesey Mere in Clare's day covered some 2,000 acres and was the habitat of water birds. It was drained in 1850 and turned into arable land.

wilding *adj.*, growing in the wild.

winnow *v.*, blow about in the breeze.

witching *adj.*, bewitching.

woodbine *n.*, honeysuckle, *Lonicera periclymenum*.

writing lark *n.*, yellow-hammer, *Emberiza citrinella*, derived from the irregular black, zig-zag lines upon the eggs, resembling writing.

yoe *n.*, ewe.

younker *n.*, youngster.

OXFORD

MORE OXFORD PAPERBACKS

This book is just one of nearly 1000 Oxford Paperbacks currently in print. If you would like details of other Oxford Paperbacks, including titles in the World's Classics, Oxford Reference, Oxford Books, OPUS, Past Masters, Oxford Authors, and Oxford Shakespeare series, please write to:

UK and Europe: Oxford Paperbacks Publicity Manager, Arts and Reference Publicity Department, Oxford University Press, Walton Street, Oxford OX2 6DP.

Customers in UK and Europe will find Oxford Paperbacks available in all good bookshops. But in case of difficulty please send orders to the Cash-with-Order Department, Oxford University Press Distribution Services, Saxon Way West, Corby, Northants NN18 9ES. Tel: 0536 741519; Fax: 0536 746337. Please send a cheque for the total cost of the books, plus £1.75 postage and packing for orders under £20; £2.75 for orders over £20. Customers outside the UK should add 10% of the cost of the books for postage and packing.

USA: Oxford Paperbacks Marketing Manager, Oxford University Press, Inc., 200 Madison Avenue, New York, N.Y. 10016.

Canada: Trade Department, Oxford University Press, 70 Wynford Drive, Don Mills, Ontario M3C 1J9.

Australia: Trade Marketing Manager, Oxford University Press, G.P.O. Box 2784Y, Melbourne 3001, Victoria.

South Africa: Oxford University Press, P.O. Box 1141, Cape Town 8000.

Oxford Reference

The Oxford Reference series offers authoritative and up-to-date reference books in paperback across a wide range of topics.

Abbreviations
Art and Artists
Ballet
Biology
Botany
Business
Card Games
Chemistry
Christian Church
Classical Literature
Computing
Dates
Earth Sciences
Ecology
English Christian
  Names
English Etymology
English Language
English Literature
English Place-Names
Eponyms
Finance
Fly-Fishing
Fowler's Modern
  English Usage
Geography
Irish Mythology
King's English
Law
Literary Guide to Great
  Britain and Ireland
Literary Terms

Mathematics
Medical Dictionary
Modern Quotations
Modern Slang
Music
Nursing
Opera
Oxford English
Physics
Popes
Popular Music
Proverbs
Quotations
Sailing Terms
Saints
Science
Ships and the Sea
Sociology
Spelling
Superstitions
Theatre
Twentieth-Century Art
Twentieth-Century
  History
Twentieth-Century
  World Biography
Weather Facts
Word Games
World Mythology
Writer's Dictionary
Zoology

THE STRUGGLE FOR
THE MASTERY OF EUROPE 1848–1918

A. J. P. Taylor

The fall of Metternich in the revolutions of 1848 heralded an era of unprecedented nationalism in Europe, culminating in the collapse of the Hapsburg, Romanov, and Hohenzollern dynasties at the end of the First World War. In the intervening seventy years the boundaries of Europe changed dramatically from those established at Vienna in 1815. Cavour championed the cause of *Risorgimento* in Italy; Bismarck's three wars brought about the unification of Germany; Serbia and Bulgaria gained their independence courtesy of the decline of Turkey—'the sick man of Europe'; while the great powers scrambled for places in the sun in Africa. However, with America's entry into the war and President Wilson's adherence to idealistic internationalist principles, Europe ceased to be the centre of the world, although its problems, still primarily revolving around nationalist aspirations, were to smash the Treaty of Versailles and plunge the world into war once more.

A. J. P. Taylor has drawn the material for his account of this turbulent period from the many volumes of diplomatic documents which have been published in the five major European languages. By using vivid language and forceful characterization, he has produced a book that is as much a work of literature as a contribution to scientific history.

'One of the glories of twentieth-century writing.'
Observer

OXFORD REFERENCE

THE CONCISE OXFORD COMPANION TO ENGLISH LITERATURE

Edited by Margaret Drabble and Jenny Stringer

Based on the immensely popular fifth edition of the *Oxford Companion to English Literature* this is an indispensable, compact guide to the central matter of English literature.

There are more than 5,000 entries on the lives and works of authors, poets, playwrights, essayists, philosophers, and historians; plot summaries of novels and plays; literary movements; fictional characters; legends; theatres; periodicals; and much more.

The book's sharpened focus on the English literature of the British Isles makes it especially convenient to use, but there is still generous coverage of the literature of other countries and of other disciplines which have influenced or been influenced by English literature.

From reviews of *The Oxford Companion to English Literature*:

'a book which one turns to with constant pleasure . . . a book with much style and little prejudice' Iain Gilchrist, *TLS*

'it is quite difficult to imagine, in this genre, a more useful publication' Frank Kermode, *London Review of Books*

'incarnates a living sense of tradition . . . sensitive not to fashion merely but to the spirit of the age' Christopher Ricks, *Sunday Times*